Middle Age

Middle Age

edited by Roger Owen

British Broadcasting Corporation

Published by the British Broadcasting Corporation
35 Marylebone High Street, London, W1M 4AA

First published 1967
Reprinted 1969

The television series Middle Age *was first broadcast in October to November 1967. Repeated on BBC 2 on Thursdays at 7.00 p.m.–7.30 p.m. from 22 May to 19 June 1969.*

Acknowledgment is due to the following:
PROFESSOR ELLIOTT JAQUES for 'The mid-life crisis' from *The International Journal of Psycho-Analysis*; DR DORIS M. ODLUM for 'Marriage and the family in middle age' from *The Royal Society of Health Journal*; JOYCE WEINER ASSOCIATES for 'A new life in middle age' by Dr Anthony Storr from *The Sunday Times*

Printed in England by Cox & Wyman Ltd,
London, Reading and Fakenham

SBN: 563 07366 7

Contents

PART 4: ROLES

PART I PERSONALITY

Middle age: an introduction

D. B. Bromley

Dr D. B. Bromley is Senior Lecturer in Psychology at the University of Liverpool and Honorary Scientific Adviser to the Medical Research Council Unit, for research on the occupational aspects of ageing. He is the author of, among other things, a recent Pelican book, *The Psychology of Human Ageing*.

There is no agreed meaning for the term 'middle age' and it is not listed in standard dictionaries or encyclopedias – middle age is a convenient fiction. The word seems to refer to a period of life which lies roughly mid-way between adolescence and old age. Both 'adolescence' and 'old age' are, by comparison with 'middle age', fairly well defined terms, although even the term 'old age' is not free from ambiguity. The reason for these differences seems to be as follows. Adolescence begins with the onset of definite biological changes known as puberty. Soon after these biological changes are complete, and soon after the individual has reached the end of the main period of growth and development, he normally changes from a position of relative dependence on the family to a position of relative independence. He becomes a 'young adult' member of society and takes on occupational, family and other responsibilities. From this time onwards, until old age is reached, the biological changes associated with increased age are gradual, relatively unobtrusive, but cumulative in their effects. Eventually, these cumulative degenerative effects encroach upon the ordinary functions of everyday life, and unless the individual dies as a consequence of injury or disease he eventually reaches a state of physical and psychological dilapidation that we refer to as senility or extreme old age.

There are differences between individuals in the age of onset of puberty and in the duration and pattern of changes associated with adolescence, but these are small compared with the wide range of individual differences in the pattern of changes associated with old age. It is the existence of a wide range of differences between individual people that makes it difficult to assign a definite chronological period even to that part of the human life cycle that we call old age. The ambiguity of the term has the consequence of making most generalizations about 'old people' or 'old age' suspect, e.g. that old age is a time of tranquillity or that old people like to be with people their own age. The term 'middle age' is more ambiguous still, since there are no reliable biological markers, except perhaps the menopause, though even the menopause is not directly or systematically related to any of the more widely accepted psychological and social characteristics of middle age.

Since Nature has not seen fit to create a definite period of middle age we are obliged to invent one. We can do this by searching for convenient or arbitrary criteria. For example, in the U.K., the age of forty, approximately, marks the beginning of the second half of the average working life of men. Among women, child bearing is usually over and the changes associated with the menopause are beginning. The average age of women in the menopause is about forty-seven. The mid-point of the post-developmental part of the human life cycle lies between forty-five and fifty years for men and a little later for women – that is to say, at this point the average man can expect to live about another twenty-five years, the average woman at age fifty–fifty-five can also expect to live about another twenty-five years. The familiar stereotype 'middle age' carries overtones of being settled, of being comfortable and established, perhaps a little delicate in health, of being experienced and mature or possibly past one's best, of being out of the rat race, and so on. These overtones are derived from commonly accepted notions about the psychological and social characteristics of the middle-aged, and, as we have already seen, since there are no reliable biological markers, and there are very wide differences between individuals, they constitute convenient, if somewhat inadequate, criteria for defining middle age. By contrast, the term middle age does not carry overtones of mental and physical dilapidation, of being retired or disengaged from the main streams of community and work activities, or of being close to death.

Thus, one might say, middle age is a state of mind, a way of feeling and thinking about oneself and one's position in the world – especially one's position relative to people a little younger or a little older than oneself. If one wanted to be more precise one could define arbitrary points in the career cycles of men and women or in the cycle of events in raising a family. It would soon become obvious that as far as defining middle age is concerned, the career patterns of airline pilots, sales representatives, politicians, journalists, members of the Armed Forces and others, have little in common, do not provide comparable markers, and permit wide variations in chronological age even among people in the same career grade. Different parents start families at different ages, they have different numbers of children, the children are spread out differently and they leave home at different ages. Hence, one cannot assert that a given chronological age is associated with any particular phase of parenthood. One could, of course, calculate statistical averages for families of various sizes and social origins, or for career patterns, but the variations between individuals would diminish the practical value of such averages.

However, although it is difficult to establish social markers which are universally valid – or even valid over a large segment of the population – this does not prevent a person from having his own private views about his biological, psychological and social status relative to other people of various chronological ages. It is possible, therefore, that it is the individual's private view of himself and the world that determines whether he is middle-aged or not. If he thinks and feels that he is 'middle-aged' he is middle-aged. In fact, few research studies have attempted to define the subjective psychological characteristics of middle age, and until more systematic investigations have been carried out the best we do is to look critically at common assumptions and expectations about 'being middle-aged'.

Since chronological age is associated with a variety of social prescriptions for behaviour and numerous social institutions – legal rights and responsibilities, voting, insurance cover, promotion, retirement, and so on – a person can scarcely help being aware of his age position relative to other people. In simpler communities, it is not unusual for an 'age set' system to operate. That is to say, individuals born in a particular period are regarded as belonging in the same age set and they move systematically and at the same times into consecutive status positions in their community. In more advanced and complex communities, the age set system breaks down towards the end of the period of full time education but is re-established at the end of the working life since a retiring age of 65 years or thereabouts is widely accepted. Although the formal age set system is too inflexible for advanced and complex societies, occupational advancement and social honours still depend to some extent on chronological age; but ability, experience, achievement and health are recognized as being more relevant to questions of promotion and prestige, and consideration of them can override or modify age norms. The particular set of facts to be taken into account when we attempt to determine our 'social age' varies from one person to another, since the circumstances surrounding a person are unique – although, no doubt, some broad similarities could be established. Writers, artists, scientists, teachers, doctors, businessmen and many others are aware of the sequence of events making up their career structure, They appreciate that there are typical ages for certain kinds of work, responsibility, pay and promotion. They know the normal age limits for the sequence of events, so they can appreciate whether they are in advance of or behind other people following the same career structure. In a similar way, a woman can appreciate whether she married relatively early or relatively late, whether her standard of living is on a par with that of her equals in age and social class, whether she is having children late in life or not, and whether she 'looks her age' or not.

In all these ways, we are able to keep a check on our progress through life, and we can often take action in an attempt to speed up or retard the process. Each person has his own frame of reference for judging his progress in life – though he usually adopts criteria similar to those of other people, since his assessment is based on his position relative to them. In this way, our appreciation of our 'social age' is an important part of our self image; being in advance of the standard rate of progress will generally lead to feelings of confidence and increased self-worth, whereas a slower than average rate of progress will generally lead to feelings of inadequacy, despondency and disappointment.

One of the dangers in this kind of self-evaluation is that the individual may have a false picture of his own abilities and personal qualities or a false picture of the general pattern of circumstances and events relevant to his position in society. He may overrate his potentialities or he may misjudge the amount of freedom he has to manipulate his life. He may not appreciate the complex constraints or the unforeseen long term consequences of his actions which help to determine the possibilities for and the limitations upon his progress. Apart from simply misunderstanding the situation, the individual may overrate, i.e. feel too strongly about, certain eventualities, such as promotion or social recognition, and suffer unnecessary feelings of guilt, anxiety, depression, anger and the like.

If middle age refers to any particular stage in life, it refers to that stage when the individual becomes aware of how the sequence and pattern of events in his life history have had long-term consequences and have culminated in a largely unalterable web of circumstances from which he can hardly escape (and, indeed, may find very much to his liking). From this time onwards the individual sees, however dimly, that the probability of shifting to a radically different pattern of life is very small, although, given the appropriate psychological characteristics (e.g. Gauguin) or situational factors (e.g. winning the Pools), massive readjustments are possible.

Although increases in chronological age between say 20 and 60 are not associated with precise and universal biological characteristics, they are associated with gradual and cumulative changes of which the average individual soon becomes aware. Among the more obvious physical signs are greying hair, loss of hair, poorer vision and hearing, loss of skin elasticity (lines, wrinkles, shadows), increased weight, and loss of teeth. Since the changes are gradual and have little effect on the ordinary activities of everyday life, most normal individuals can adapt to (learn to live with) these changes, and provided they are slight they may have little effect on the person's self-image or on his personal adjustment and social relationships. In time, however, the effects are so substantial that the individual can no longer regard himself as 'young' in the biological sense, and when this recognition is forced upon him it initiates changes in his self-image and in his relationships with other people. Even this recognition is not usually abrupt and complete in its effects. More often than not, it is a gradual realization of one's changing relationships with other people; it leads to the abandonment of some attitudes and activities and the adoption of others that seem to be more appropriate to one's age, health and social position. Most prominent, perhaps, among these changes are those affecting the formation of friendships and leisure time interests and activities. Naturally, chronological age as such is not the critical factor, since chronological age records only the passage of time since one's birth. The critical factor is rather the set of social prescriptions and personal beliefs about what is appropriate for people of a given age, e.g. that one's friends should be in the same age bracket and that activities such as driving sports cars, playing bowls, or attending evening classes in weight training are suitable for one age group but not for another. Even here, the social prescriptions are often vague and weak and some individuals can, without too much difficulty or embarrassment, make friends outside the 'normal' range for people of their age or take part in activities which others think inappropriate for people their age. There is, perhaps, too much emphasis on age segregation in the U.K. and we might do better to emulate the Americans who appear to be willing to have people of widely different ages participating in their varied community activities. One might even go so far as to deprecate the movement to establish clubs and centres for old people on the grounds that many old people have little in common except their advanced chronological age. They should be encouraged and given opportunities to participate in social organizations dealing with special interests – politics, welfare, athletics, charity, education and so on. One of the problems, of course, is that many men and women reach the age of retirement without ever having cultivated leisure time activities or special interests and they find it difficult to occupy themselves during their waking hours. The movement towards 'preparation for retirement' is to be encouraged since it could do a great deal to prevent or minimize some of the more obvious disadvantages of life after sixty-five. Such preparation for retirement should begin some five or ten years before retirement is due, and it may be useful to think of 'pre-retirement' as a small segment of the human life cycle separating the end of middle age from the beginning of the phases of retirement and old age. Alternatively, one could regard the pre-retirement phase as equivalent to late middle age.

It is obvious that assigning names to, and describing, stages in the human life cycle is largely a matter of convenience and definition. A self-employed person, for example, may choose not to retire at all or to retire late in life; so that the chronological ages marking his late middle age or pre-retirement period of life would be different from those of say a teacher, in poor health, who is considering early retirement. Preparation for retirement involves not merely the individual himself and his immediate family, but also those occupational, recreational, financial, health and welfare organizations which affect and are affected by the individual and others like him. A better understanding of the facts of middle and old age among the public at large might do much to encourage more positive action to alleviate the burdens of later life – for example through preventive medicine, improved welfare and financial provisions, the abolition of indefensible age limits in occupational and other spheres of life, more community activities, and the encouragement of older people to maintain their interest and participation in social organizations with special interests. Since it is usual for the authority in social organizations to be held by middle-aged and elderly people, it will be necessary to ensure that their continued presence does not have adverse effects upon such organizations.

Although the majority of people over the age of 20 grow older gradually (if not always gracefully) and evolve appropriate strategies of adjustment to cope with their changed health and circumstances, yet for a number of people one or other of the pathological changes which become increasingly common as age increases may appear suddenly with dramatic consequences on the person's style of life. Among the more striking of these pathological conditions are psychiatric illness, cancer, bronchitis, heart disease and sensory impairments. These, and other less disabling conditions may oblige the individual (and those associated with him) to make radical alterations in his schedule of life activities. It may be one such disaster which convinces the individual that he has left one stage of life and entered another, though, naturally, people react differently to the same event – one minister of religion, advised by his doctor to take up golf following his recovery from a heart condition in early middle age, found that golf was better than Unitarianism! Normally, however, the occurrence of pathological conditions and the normal effects of ageing have adverse effects on health, vigour and life activities, leading to restrictions on outlook and endeavour.

Because the adverse biological changes of middle life are gradual and widely recognized (if not well understood), it is not surprising that many people evolve special ways of dealing with them. Systematic attempts to prevent or retard the changes are common – the individual becomes more sensitive to bodily dysfunction and the risks of injury and infection. He may react in various ways – by regulating his diet and by exercising, by recourse to patent medicines and quack treatments, by consulting his doctor more readily, by talking about health problems with other people (conversation in the middle years readily turns to questions of weight and health). Among women, excess fat, lines and wrinkles, varicose veins and sundry other undesirable signs of ageing elicit various reactions – courses in slimming (sensible or useless), heavier expenditure on cosmetics and beauty treatment, greater interest in magazine or newspaper articles on health, and so on. In the U.K., perhaps more than elsewhere, such reactions are usually fairly discreet and shortlived – discreet in the sense that the individual tends to keep the emotional aspects of the problems largely to himself, and shortlived in the sense that, since many if not most of the preventive and remedial measures are unscientific and ineffective (e.g. rejuvenation), the individual usually becomes reconciled to the biological facts of middle age and to the changed psychological and social characteristics that follow such changes. A few predisposed individuals will become hypochrondriacal since there will be an ample number of minor symptoms upon which their anxiety can focus – headaches, skin disorders and so on. Others unwilling to face the facts will deny or do nothing about quite obvious danger signals, thus delaying diagnosis and treatment and perhaps diminishing their chances of recovery.

The insistent claims of the body on the attention of the person eventually produce alterations in the person's attitude to and care of his body. This is not a bad thing since there are good reasons for supposing that the physical health of most people is well below what it could be with proper diet, exercise and medical attention. Unfortunately, public ignorance about elementary human biology and the effects of ageing often produces ineffective reactions. The widespread consumption of alcohol, cigarettes and sugar probably has adverse effects; the unnatural conditions, activities and postures of modern living may also contribute their adverse effects. It is interesting to observe that the main factor leading to an increased expectation of life in recent years has been the improvement in infant and child health; it may be that systematic attempts to improve physical health in the middle years would lead to a similar, though probably not so great, extension of the active span of human life. One way to approach this problem would be through health education and greater emphasis on preventive measures.

When the person is obliged to admit to a marked reduction in his biological capacities (from a previous high or fairly stable level) or, more usually, as he *gradually* admits to reductions in his biological capacities, he adopts a changed view of himself – as being no longer attractive to members of the opposite sex, as needing or having to avoid special kinds of food or recreation, as running risks of one sort or another, as having done his stint, and of being predisposed to certain symptoms – stomach upsets, headaches and so on – which serve partly as devices for scheduling his own activities and partly as devices for manipulating others.

The middle-aged person's increased vulnerability to physical (and mental) ill health contrasts with the security of his social position, which usually reaches a maximum in this period. Systematic studies of the ages at which people hold positions of power and prestige or receive high incomes show that the period covers, roughly, the years from the early forties to the late sixties – depending upon the kind of activity considered. By definition, only a few individuals succeed in reaching the pinnacles of their profession, so many aspirants must eventually readjust themselves to the fact that they have reached the limit of their particular career progress. For some, coming to terms with the facts may be hard and long delayed and may be accompanied by a good deal of emotional upset, but the majority probably accept their position with good grace.

Professional competence in middle age is not so much a matter of inherited ability as of acquired skills and knowledge. It means having learned the 'rules' of the particular professional 'games' we are required to play, of knowing *what* to say and do, *how* to say it or do it, and *whom* to deal with. By the time he reaches the middle and late forties a professional person, politician or businessman has usually acquired a complex set of techniques for scheduling his daily activities. He has a firm set of personal values by means of which he judges how much time, effort and money he should devote to each endeavour; these values dictate priorities broadly, e.g. family versus job, holidays versus domestic appliances, and in detail, e.g. his decisions about the organization of the activities related to his job. In other words, he has acquired a firm set of values, attitudes and basic assumptions, which act as premises guiding his daily decisions and actions – he has a 'behaviour policy'. He may find it difficult to make this policy explicit, but it is there nevertheless, and can be discovered by suitable techniques of observation and interrogation. This policy or strategy is not necessarily the most efficient one, but, for most individuals, it represents a solution, gradually evolved over many years, to the problem of how to deploy one's limited time and resources to cope with a variety of necessary and optional conditions of life – such as a sick wife, an expanding business, professional competition, children, and the like.

The rate of change of the individual's circumstances is generally slower and the flow of events has shaped his activities and surroundings to a fairly definite pattern. The web of circumstances and possibilities constrains the person's behaviour, and these constraints have more of a 'demand' character, i.e. are more compelling in their effects, than those of earlier life, although undoubtedly some middle-aged people feel constrained by circumstances which are imaginary or at least overestimated – for example, with regard to occupational mobility, marital ties or leisure time pusuits.

If one regards 'middle age' in part as that period of life which forms the plateau or steady state between early adult life and the pre-retirement period, then the attainment of it provides many opportunities for revaluation. At this time, the individual is often privately more aware of the changes in his biological health and psychological capacities than those around him, since he has more opportunities to perceive such changes. He will almost certainly be making all kinds of comparisons between himself and others who are older or younger than he is. He begins to calculate his age rather than remember it automatically. He begins, if he is reflective enough, to see his life in the perspective of social history – the depression, the pre-war years, World War II, the cold war – as well as in terms of events and relationships involving individual people. He reviews the high points and low points of his life, the fortunes and the misfortunes, the mistakes and the achievements, the opportunities taken or missed, and the obstacles – overcome or not. All this is not merely reminiscence – it is an active process of self examination, of reinterpreting his past and re-estimating his position and potential with a view to learning the correct lessons from the past and choosing the correct ends and means for the future. At this time of life our retrospective view of life determines our prospect – rather as if the place we had reached on a trek was being used as a vantage point to work out how we had arrived and how we might proceed. Thus we sometimes get, in middle age, a revaluation of ourselves – our ways of behaving, our relationships with other people, our interests, values and activities. Such revaluation may be followed by changes in behaviour and beliefs, depending upon whether we want to alter or to become reconciled to the disadvantages in our lives. This is not to say that middle age is the only time of life when we take stock of our position – obviously, it is a continuous process. But, because of the growing limitations on *choice* and the greater weight of evidence about ourselves and our circumstances, there is more inclination to set terminal goals, to abandon aims which are improbable of accomplishment, to settle for what is reasonable, to come to terms with life. In the later stages of this kind of reassessment and revaluation, there begins the middle-aged person's greater reliance upon his subordinates or his children in a kind of 'phasing out' of his aims and responsibilities. His orientation in time shifts more frequently from 'How long have I lived?' to 'How long have I to live?' for, together with material and other constraints, there are obvious limitations upon what he can reasonably expect to do in the time that is left. Naturally, this awareness of what is 'reasonable' alters one's motivation, since, as far as occupation and social relationships are concerned, it is the prospect of benefits of one sort or another that act as the incentive – the spur – to action. If the prospect changes – as indeed it must – then the motives which instigate, sustain and direct behaviour must also change – although, because of emotional factors in our make-up, we are not always as rational in our motivations and reorientations in middle age as perhaps we should be. Whether this has any connexion with the increased susceptibility to emotional disorders in middle and later life is not known.

Surprisingly little is known about the long term relationships between development and ageing; we can only speculate about preventive and remedial measures to counteract the adverse changes – for example, as to whether preventing intellectual functions from falling into disuse would retard the normal processes of intellectual decline. The normal relationships between ageing and intellectual creativity are well-established, but for all we know these relationships might be changed by altering the social conditions in which intellectual creativity takes place. Age changes in personality are much less obvious than age changes in creativity or in human physiology, and the methodological difficulties of studying personality changes are more substantial. Moreover, the normal concepts and methods of studying personality are not very satisfactory for investigating what appear to be important aspects of individual adjustment in middle and late life, so new concepts and new methods need to be developed. Among the topics we can expect to see investigated in the near future are, for example, the effects of age during the middle years on: confidence, professional competence, the perception of age in oneself and others, interpersonal relationships, adjustment to common occurrences in middle age (bereavement, redundancy, departure of children, etc.), the perception of time, the self image, sleep, sexual behaviour, emotional stress and maladjustment. Other areas of research are likely to include: cross cultural and social class comparisons of middle age, sex differences and similarities during the middle years.

In summary: the term 'middle age' is at present ambiguous, although it is possible to establish arbitrary definitions and criteria which at least have the effect of clarifying some interesting and important issues. Broadly speaking, middle age is the period falling between the 'young adult' and the 'pre-retirement' phases of the human life cycle, and one could, if necessary, calculate statistical averages to show the calendar ages at which people could expect to reach certain stages in their careers and in their family life. The middle years are associated, in general, with gradual but cumulative adverse biological changes to which the individual has to adjust. Some individuals are faced with serious problems of re-adjustment following an abrupt change for the worse in their physical or mental health. As a result of the normal and pathological changes in human biology during the middle years, there occurs a variety of complex psychological and social consequences with tremendous differences between individuals. The person is sometimes (not always) privately more aware of the age changes than the people around him, and it is common for people to make comparisons between themselves and others in order to check their 'social age'. Such comparisons may contribute to or diminish the individual's feelings of self worth and inner satisfaction and help to determine, together with the individual's self assessment of his physical health, whether he thinks and feels that he is middle-aged – this is perhaps the main psychological criterion of middle age. Gradually, the middle-aged person is caught in a web of circumstances and events which permits few possibilities for change; hence, he may use opportunities to reconsider his position and to reorient his life while he can. He learns a complex set of strategies and tactics of personal adjustment to cope with predictable events in his circumstances. Unfortunately, at the present time, we have little reliable scientific information about middle age, and there appears to be a great deal of public ignorance and misunderstanding about this part of the life cycle. More research, improvements in preventive and remedial measures (of various sorts) and better dissemination of the facts can be expected to have beneficial effects.

The mid-life crisis

Elliott Jaques

Professor Elliott Jacques was educated at the University of Toronto, the Johns Hopkins Medical School and Harvard. He qualified as a psycho-analyst at the British Psycho-Analytical Society, and is a practising psycho-analyst. In 1948 he led a research team for the Tavistock Institute of Human Relations, and has continued privately as a social analytic consultant. He is an adviser to the Ministry of Health and Board of Trade. Currently he is head of the School of Social Sciences at Brunel University.

In the course of the development of the individual there are critical phases which have the character of change points, or periods of rapid transition. Less familiar perhaps, though nonetheless real, are the crises which occur around the age of 35 – which I shall term the mid-life crisis – and at full maturity around the age of 65. It is the mid-life crisis with which I shall deal in this article.

When I say that the mid-life crisis occurs around the age of 35, I mean that it takes place in the middle thirties, that the process of transition runs on for some years, and that the exact period will vary among individuals. The transition is often obscured in women by the proximity of the onset of changes connected with the menopause. In the case of men, the change has from time to time been referred to as the male climacteric, because of the reduction in the intensity of sexual behaviour which often occurs at that time.

Crisis in genius

I first became aware of this period as a critical stage in development when I noticed a marked tendency towards crisis in the creative work of great men in their middle and late thirties. It is clearly expressed by Richard Church in his autobiography *The Voyage Home*:

> 'There seems to be a biological reason for men and women, when they reach the middle thirties, finding themselves beset with misgivings, agonizing inquiries, and a loss of zest. Is it that state which the medieval schoolmen called *accidie*, the cardinal sin of spiritual sloth? I believe it is.'

This crisis may express itself in three different ways: the creative career may simply come to an end, either in a drying-up of creative work, or in actual death; the creative capacity may begin to show and express itself for the first time; or a decisive change in the quality and content of creativeness may take place.

Perhaps the most striking phenomenon is what happens to the death rate among creative artists. I had got the impression that the age of 37 seemed to figure pretty prominently in the death of individuals of this category. This impression was upheld by taking a random sample of some 310 painters, composers, poets, writers, and sculptors, of undoubted greatness or of genius. The death rate shows a sudden jump between 35 and 39, at which period it is much above the normal death rate. The group includes Mozart, Raphael, Chopin, Rimbaud, Purcell, Baudelaire, Watteau. . . . There is then a big drop below the normal death rate between the ages of 40 and 44, followed by a return to the normal death rate pattern in the late forties. The closer one keeps to genius in the sample, the more striking and clearcut is this spiking of the death rate in mid-life.

The change in creativity which occurs during this period can be seen in the lives of countless artists. Bach, for example, was mainly an organist until his cantorship at Leipzig at 38, at which time he began his colossal achievements as a composer. Rossini's life is described in the following terms:

> 'His comparative silence during the period 1832–1868 (i.e. from 40 to his death at 74) makes his biography like the

narrative of two lives – swift triumph, and a long life of seclusion.'

Racine had thirteen years of continuous success culminating in *Phèdre* at the age of 38; he then produced nothing for some twelve years. The characteristic work of Goldsmith, Constable, and Goya emerged between the ages of 35 and 38. By the age of 43 Ben Jonson had produced all the plays worthy of his genius, although he lived to be 64. At 33 Gauguin gave up his job in a bank, and by 39 had established himself in his creative career as a painter. Donatello's work after 39 is described by a critic as showing a marked change in style, in which he departed from the statuesque balance of his earlier work and turned to the creation of an almost instantaneous expression of life.

Goethe, between the ages of 37 and 39, underwent a profound change in outlook, associated with his trip to Italy. As many of his biographers have pointed out, the importance of this journey and this period in his life cannot be exaggerated. He himself regarded it as the climax to his life. Never before had he gained such complete understanding of his genius and mission as a poet. His work then began to reflect the classical spirit of Greek tragedy and of the Renaissance.

Michelangelo carried out a series of masterpieces until he was 40: his 'David' was finished at 29, the decoration of the roof of the Sistine Chapel at 37, and his 'Moses' between 37 and 40. During the next fifteen years little is known of any artistic work. There was a creative lull until, at 55, he began to work on the great Medici monument and then later on 'The Last Judgement' and frescoes in the Pauline Chapel.

Let me make it clear that I am not suggesting that the careers of most creative persons either begin or end during the mid-life crisis. There are few creative geniuses who live and work into maturity, in whom the quality of greatness cannot be discerned in early adulthood in the form either of created works or of the potential for creating them: Beethoven Shakespeare, Goethe, Couperin, Ibsen, Balzac, Voltaire, Verdi,

Handel, Goya, Dürer, to name but a very few at random. But there are equally few in whom a decisive change cannot be seen in the quality of their work – in whose work the effects of their having gone through a mid-life crisis cannot be discerned. The reactions range all the way from severe and dramatic crisis, to a smoother and less troubled transition – just as reactions to the phase of adolescent crisis may range from severe disturbance and breakdown to relatively ordered readjustment to mental and sexual adulthood – but the effects of the change are there to be discerned. What then are the main features of this change?

There are two features which seem to me of outstanding importance. One of these has to do with the mode of work; the second has to do with the content of the work. Let me consider each of these in turn. I shall use the phrase 'early adulthood' for the pre-mid-life phase, and 'mature adulthood' for the post-mid-life phase.

Change in mode of work

I can best describe the change in mode of work which I have in mind by describing the extreme of its manifestation. The creativity of the twenties and the early thirties tends to be a hot-from-the-fire creativity. It is intense and spontaneous, and comes out ready-made. The spontaneous effusions of Mozart, Keats, Shelley, Rimbaud, are the prototype. Most of the work seems to go on unconsciously. The conscious production is rapid, the pace of creation often being dictated by the limits of the artist's capacity physically to record the words or music he is expressing.

A vivid description of early adult type of work is given in Gittings' biography of Keats:

> 'Keats all this year had been living on spiritual capital. He had used and spent every experience almost as soon as it had come into his possession, every sight, person, book, emotion or thought had been converted spontaneously

> into poetry. Could he or any other poet have lasted at such a rate? . . . He could write no more by these methods. He realized this himself when he wished to compose as he said 'without fever'. He could not keep this high pulse beating and endure.'

By contrast, the creativity of the late thirties and after is a sculpted creativity. The inspiration may be hot and intense. The unconscious work is no less than before. But there is a big step between the first effusion of inspiration and the finished created product. The inspiration itself may come more slowly. Even if there are sudden bursts of inspiration, they are only the beginning of the work process. The initial inspiration must first be externalized in its elemental state. Then begins the process of forming and fashioning the external product, by means of working and re-working the externalized material. I use the term sculpting because the nature of the sculptor's material – it is the sculptor working in stone of whom I am thinking – forces him into this kind of relationship with the product of his creative imagination. There occurs a process of interplay between unconscious intuitive work and inspiration, and the considered perception of the externally emergent creation and the reaction to it.

In her note 'A Character Trait of Freud's', Joan Riviere describes Freud's exhorting her in connexion with some psycho-analytic idea which had occurred to her:

> 'Write it, write it, put it down in black and white . . . get it out, produce it, make something of it – *outside you*, that is; give it an existence independently of you.'

This externalizing process is part of the essence of work in mature adulthood, when, as in the case of Freud, the initially externalized material is not itself the end product, or nearly the end product, but is rather the starting point, the object of further working over, modification, elaboration, sometimes for periods of years.

In distinguishing between the precipitate creativity of early adulthood and the sculpted creativity of mature adulthood, I do not want to give the impression of drawing a hard and fast line between the two phases. There are of course times when a creative person in mature adulthood will be subject to bursts of inspiration and rapid-fire creative production. Equally there will be found instances of mature and sculpted creative work done in early adulthood. The 'David' of Michelangelo is, I think, the supreme example of the latter.

But the instances where work in early adulthood has the sculpted and worked-over quality are rare. Sometimes, as in scientific work, there may be the appearance of sculpted work. Young physicists in their twenties, for example, may produce startling discoveries, which are the result of continuous hard work and experimentation. But these discoveries result from the application of modern theories about the structure of matter – theories which themselves have been the product of the sculpted work of mature adulthood of such geniuses as Thomson and Einstein.

Equally, genuinely creative work in mature adulthood may sometimes not appear to be externally worked over and sculpted, and yet actually be so. What seems to be rapid and unworked-over creation is commonly the reworking of themes which have been worked upon before, or which may have been slowly emerging over the years in previous works. We need look no farther than the work of Freud for a prime example of this process of books written rapidly, which are nevertheless the coming to fruition of ideas which have been worked upon, fashioned, reformulated, left incomplete and full of loose ends, and then reformulated once again in a surging forward through the emergence of new ideas for overcoming previous difficulties.

The reality of the distinction comes out in the fact that certain materials are more readily applicable to the precipitate creativity of early adulthood than are others. Thus, for example, musical composition, lyrical poetry, are much more amenable to rapid creative production than are sculpting in stone or painting in oils. It is noteworthy, therefore, that whereas there are very many poets and composers who achieve greatness in early adulthood – indeed in their early twenties or their late teens – there are very few sculptors or painters in oils who do so. With oil paint and stone, the working relationship to the materials themselves is of importance, and demands that the creative process should go through the stage of initial externalization and working-over of the externalized product. The written word and musical notation do not of necessity have this same plastic external objective quality. They can be sculpted and worked over, but they can also readily be treated merely as a vehicle for the immediate recording of unconsciously articulated products which are brought forward whole and complete – or nearly so.

Quality and content of creativity

The change in mode of work, then, between early and mature adulthood, is a change from precipitate to sculpted creativity. Let me now consider for a moment the change in the quality and content of the creativity. The change I have in mind is the emergence of a tragic and philosophical content which then moves on to serenity in the creativity of mature adulthood, in contrast to a more characteristically lyrical and descriptive content to the work of early adulthood. This distinction is a commonly held one, and may perhaps be considered sufficiently self-evident to require little explication or argument. It is implied, of course, in my choice of the adjectives 'early' and 'mature' to qualify the two phases of adulthood which I am discussing.

The change may be seen in the more human, tragic and less fictitious and stage quality of Dickens's writing from *David Copperfield* (which he wrote at 37) onwards. It may be seen also in the transition in Shakespeare from the historical plays and comedies to the tragedies. When he was about 31, in the midst of writing his lyrical comedies, he produced *Romeo and Juliet*. The great series of tragedies and Roman plays, however, began to appear a few years later; *Julius Caesar*, *Hamlet*,

Othello, *King Lear*, and *Macbeth* are believed to have been written most probably between the ages of 35 and 40.

There are many familiar features of the change in question. Late adolescent and early adult idealism and optimism accompanied by split-off and projected hate, are given up and supplanted by a more contemplative pessimism. There is a shift from radical desire and impatience to a more reflective and tolerant conservatism. Beliefs in the inherent goodness of man are replaced by a recognition and acceptance of the fact that inherent goodness is accompanied by hate and destructive forces within, which contribute to man's own misery and tragedy. To the extent that hate, destruction, and death are found explicitly in early adult creativeness, they enter in the form of the satanic or the macabre, as in Poe and in Baudelaire, and not as worked-through and resolved anxieties.

The spirit of early adult creativeness is summed up in Shelley's *Prometheus Unbound*. In her notes on this work, Shelley's wife has written:

> 'The prominent feature of Shelley's theory of the destiny of the human species is that evil is not inherent in the system of the Creation, but an accident that might be expelled . . . God made Earth and Man perfect, till he by his fall 'brought death into the world, and all our woe'. Shelley believed that mankind had only to will that there should be no evil in the world and there would be none. . . . He was attached to this idea with fervent enthusiasm.'

This early adult idealism is built upon the *denial* of two fundamental features of human life – the inevitableness of eventual death, and the existence of hate and destructive impulses inside each person.

It is when death and human destructiveness – that is to say, both death and the death instinct – are taken into account, that the quality and content of creativity change to the tragic, reflective, and philosophical.

The successful outcome of mature creative work lies in constructive resignation both to the imperfections of men and to shortcomings in one's own work. It is this constructive resignation that then imparts serenity to life and work.

The divine comedy

I have taken these examples from creative genius because I believe the essence of the mid-life crisis is revealed in its most full and rounded form in the lives of the great. It will have become manifest that the crisis is a depressive crisis, in contrast to the adolescent crisis, which tends to be a paranoid-schizoid one.

This theme of working through depression is magnificently expressed in *The Divine Comedy*. This masterpiece of all time was begun by Dante following his banishment from Florence at the age of 37. In the opening stanzas he creates his setting in words of great power and tremendous psychological depth. He begins:

> 'In the middle of the journey of our life, I came to myself within a dark wood where the straight way was lost. Ah, how hard it is to tell of that wood, savage and harsh and dense, the thought of which renews my fear. So bitter is it that death is hardly more.'

These words have been variously interpreted; for example, as an allegorical reference to the entrance to Hell, or as a reflection of the poet's state of mind on being forced into exile, homeless and hungry for justice. They may, however, be interpreted at a deeper level as the opening scene of a vivid and perfect description of the emotional crisis of the mid-life phase, a crisis which would have gripped the mind and soul of the poet whatever his religious outlook, or however settled or unsettled his external affairs. The evidence for this conclusion exists in the fact that during the years of his early thirties which preceded his exile, he had already begun his transformation from the idyllic outlook of the *Vita Nuova* (age 27–29) through a conversion to 'philosophy' which he allegorized in the *Convivio* written when he was between 36 and 38 years of age.

Even taken quite literally, *The Divine Comedy* is a description of the poet's first full and worked-through conscious encounter with death. He is led through hell and purgatory by his master Virgil, eventually to find his own way, guided by his beloved Beatrice, into paradise. His final rapturous and mystical encounter with the being of God, represented to him in strange and abstract terms, was not mere rapture, not simply a being overwhelmed by a mystical oceanic feeling. It was a much more highly organized experience. It was expressly a vision of supreme love and knowledge, with control of impulse and of will, which promulgates the mature life of greater ease and contemplation.

> 'What is not found in the 'Paradiso', for it is foreign to the spirit of Dante, is flight from the world, absolute refuge in God, asceticism. He does not seek to fly from the world, but to instruct it, correct it, and reform it . . . he knew the world and its doings and passions.'

Awareness of personal death

Although I have thus far taken my examples from the extremes of genius, my main theme is that the mid-life crisis is a reaction which not only occurs in creative genius, but manifests itself in some form in everyone. What then is the psychological nature of this reaction to the mid-life situation, and how is it to be explained?

The simple fact of the situation is the arrival at the midpoint of life. What is simple from the point of view of chronology, however, is not simple psychologically. The individual has stopped growing up, and has begun to grow old. A new set of external circumstances has to be met. The first phase of adult life has been lived. Family and occupation have become established (or ought to have become established unless the individual's adjustment has gone seriously awry); parents have grown old, and children are at the threshold of adulthood. Youth and childhood are past and gone, and demand to be mourned. The achievement of mature and independent adulthood presents itself as the main psychological task. The paradox is that of entering the prime of life, the stage of fulfilment, but at the same time the prime and fulfilment are dated. Death lies beyond.

I believe that it is this fact of the entry upon the psychological scene of the reality and inevitability of one's own eventual personal death, that is the central and crucial feature of the mid-life phase – the feature which precipitates the critical nature of the period. Death – at the conscious level – instead of being a general conception, or an event experienced in terms of the loss of someone else, becomes a personal matter, one's own death, one's own real and actual mortality. As Freud has so accurately described the matter:

> 'We were prepared to maintain that death was the necessary outcome of life. . . . In reality, however, we were accustomed to behave as if it were otherwise. We displayed an unmistakable tendency to 'shelve' death, to eliminate it from life. We tried to hush it up. . . . That is our own death, of course. . . . No-one believes in his own death. . . . In the unconscious everyone is convinced of his own immortality.'

This attitude towards life and death, written by Freud in another context, aptly expresses the situation which we all encounter in mid-life. The reality of one's own personal death forces itself upon our attention and can no longer so readily be shelved. A 36-year-old patient, who had been in analysis for seven years and was in the course of working through a deep depressive reaction which heralded the final phase of his analysis some eighteen months later, expressed the matter with great clarity. 'Up till now,' he said, 'life has seemed an endless upward slope, with nothing but the distant horizon in view. Now suddenly I seem to have reached the crest of the hill, and there stretching ahead is the downward slope with the end of the road in sight – far enough away it's true – but there is death observably present at the end.'

From that point on this patient's plans and ambitions took

on a different hue. For the first time in his life he saw his future as circumscribed. He began his adjustment to the fact that he would not be able to accomplish in the span of a single lifetime everything he had desired to do. He could achieve only a finite amount. Much would have to remain unfinished and unrealized.

This perspective on the finitude of life was accompanied by a greater solidity and robustness in his outlook, and introduced a new quality of earthly resignation. It reflected a diminishing of his unconscious wish for immortality. Such ideas are commonly lived out in terms of denial of mourning and death, or in terms of ideas of immortality, from notions of reincarnation and life after death, to notions of longevity like those expressed by the successful 28-year-old novelist who writes in his diary, 'I shall be the most serious of men, and I shall live longer than any man.'

Dealing with the crisis

A person who reaches mid-life, either without having successfully established himself in marital and occupational life, or having established himself by means of manic activity and denial with consequent emotional impoverishment, is badly prepared for meeting the demands of middle age, and getting enjoyment out of his maturity. In such cases, the mid-life crisis, and the adult encounter with the conception of life to be lived in the setting of an approaching personal death, will likely be experienced as a period of psychological disturbance and depressive breakdown. Or breakdown may be avoided by means of a strengthening of manic defences, with a warding off of depression and persecution about ageing and death, but with an accumulation of persecutory anxiety to be faced when the inevitability of ageing and death eventually demands recognition.

The compulsive attempts, in many men and women reaching middle age, to remain young, the hypochondriacal concern over health and appearance, the emergence of sexual promiscuity in order to prove youth and potency, the hollowness and lack of genuine enjoyment of life, and the frequency of religious concern, are familiar patterns. They are attempts at a race against time. And in addition to the impoverishment of emotional life contained in the foregoing activities, real character deterioration is always possible. Retreat from psychic reality encourages intellectual dishonesty, and a weakening of moral fibre and of courage. Increase in arrogance, and ruthlessness concealing pangs of envy – or self-effacing humbleness and weakness concealing fantasies of omnipotence – are symptomatic of such change.

These defensive fantasies are equally as persecuting, however, as the chaotic and hopeless internal situation they are meant to mitigate. They lead to attempts at easy success, at a continuation on a false note of the early adult lyricism and precipitate creation – that is, creation which, by avoiding contemplation, now seeks not to express but to avoid contact with the infantile experience of hate and of death. Instead of creative enhancement by the introduction of the genuinely tragic, there is emotional impoverishment – a recoil away from creative development. As Freud incisively remarked: 'Life loses in interest, when the highest stake in the game, life itself, may not be risked.' Here is the Achilles heel of much young genius.

Second half

The last half of life can be lived with conscious knowledge of eventual death, and acceptance of this knowledge, as an integral part of living. Mourning for the dead self can begin, alongside the mourning and re-establishment of the lost objects and the lost childhood and youth. The sense of life's continuity may be strengthened. The gain is in the deepening of awareness, understanding and self-realization. Genuine values can be cultivated – of wisdom, fortitude and courage, deeper capacity for love and affection and human insight, and hopefulness and enjoyment – qualities whose genuineness stems from integration based upon the more immediate and self-conscious awareness and acceptance not only of one's own shortcomings but of one's destructive impulses, and from the greater capacity for sublimation which accompanies true resignation and detachment.

Out of the working-through of the depressive position, there is further strengthening of the capacity to accept and tolerate conflict and ambivalence. One's work need no longer be experienced as perfect. It can be worked and reworked, but it will be accepted as having shortcomings. The sculpting process can be carried on far enough so that the work is good enough. There is no need for obsessional attempts at perfection, because inevitable imperfection is no longer felt as bitter persecuting failure. Out of this mature resignation comes the serenity in the work of genius, true serenity, serenity which transcends imperfection by accepting it.

Because of the greater integration within the internal world, and a deepening of the sense of reality, a freer interaction can occur between the internal and the external worlds. Sculpted creativity expresses this freedom with its flow of inspiration from inside to outside and back, constantly repeated, again, and yet again. There is a quality of depth in mature creativity which stems from constructive resignation and detachment. Death is not infantile persecution and chaos. Life and the world go on, and we can live on in our children, our loved objects, our works, if not in immortality.

The sculpting process in creativity is facilitated because the preparation for the final phase in reality-testing has begun – the reality-testing of the end of life. For everyone, the on-coming years of the forties are the years when new starts are coming to an end. This feeling can be observed to arise in a particularly poignant way by the mid-forties. This sense of there being no more changing is anticipated in the mid-life crisis. What is begun has to be finished. Important things that the individual would have liked to achieve, would have desired to become, would have longed to have, will not be realized. The awareness of on-coming frustration is especially intense. That is why, for example, the issue of resignation is of such importance. It is resignation in the sense of conscious and unconscious acceptance of inevitable frustration on the grand scale of life as a whole.

This reality-testing is the more severe the greater is the creative ability of the individual, for the time scale of creative work increases dramatically with ability. Thus the experience is particularly painful in genius, capable of achieving vastly more than it is possible to achieve in the remaining years, and therefore frustrated by the immense vision of things to be done which will not be done. And because the route forward has become a cul-de-sac, attention begins its Proustian process of turning to the past, working it over consciously in the present, and weaving it into the concretely limited future. This consonance of past and present is a feature of much mature adult sculpting work.

The positive creativeness and the tone of serenity which accompany the successful endurance of this frustration, are characteristic of the mature production of Beethoven, Goethe, Virgil, Dante, and other giants. It is the spirit of the 'Paradiso', which ends in words of strong and quiet confidence:

> 'But now my desire and will, like a wheel that spins with even motion, were revolved by the Love that moves the sun and other stars.'

It is this spirit, on a smaller scale, which overcomes the crisis of middle life, and lives through to the enjoyment of mature creativeness and work in full awareness of death which lies beyond – resigned but not defeated.

A new life in middle age

Anthony Storr

Anthony Storr was born in 1920 and educated at Winchester College and Christ's College, Cambridge, where he studied medicine. After qualifying as a doctor in 1944 he specialized in psychiatry and held posts at Runwell Mental Hospital and at the Maudsley Hospital. He also trained as an analyst in the school of C. G. Jung, though he prefers not to be labelled as an adherent to any one analytical school. He has contributed reviews and articles to many papers including the *New Statesman*, the *Observer*, the *Sunday Times* and *New Society*, and is the author of, among other things, two Pelican books, *The Integrity of Personality* and *Sexual Deviation*.

Among those who reflect upon the human condition in our Western society, it is increasingly recognized that the decade from thirty-five to forty-five is a time of crucial importance for the development of the individual. It is a period when new possibilities emerge and new patterns of living are explored. It is also a time when emotional disturbances of many varieties are likely to be made manifest.

The comparable neglect which psychologists and educationalists have accorded this particular phase of life is the result of a prejudice which we are only now beginning to overcome. In former generations it was assumed that, by the age of forty, men and women were so fixed in their ways that little change could be expected in them. All that could be generally anticipated was an increasing mellowness and tranquillity, together with a slow decline in vigour and a more rapid decrease in both ambition and sexual interest.

This stereotype, which we have now abandoned, was reinforced by the initial discoveries of Freud. Psychoanalysis has rightly emphasized the great importance of the first five years of life in shaping the future destiny of the individual. But this insistence upon childhood development has given the impression that, by the age of thirty-five or so, a person must have reached such maturity as the vicissitudes of his childhood have allowed him, and that little further development can therefore be expected. This impression was reinforced by the reluctance of the early psychoanalysts to treat any but young patients; a practice which has since been considerably modified. Even the assumption that the ability to learn new material declines before senility sets in has been questioned in recent years; and it seems probable that, as usual, we have under-estimated our own capacities in this respect as in many others.

One reason why we are at last paying more attention to the middle years of life is the fact that so many more of us survive to reach them. We live in a society in which the proportion of elderly persons in the population is steadily increasing. This has had the effect of altering our subjective image of what is 'old' and what is 'young'. We have now postponed the age at which we conceive psychological maturity to be possible to a time of life which, in former generations, would have been assumed to be a period of decline.

A century and a half ago, age was viewed very differently. Readers of 'Emma', for example, may need to be reminded that the sagacious and equable Mr Knightley, who seems to us long since to have abandoned both youth and indiscretion, is only 'about seven- or eight-and-thirty' at the beginning of Jane Austen's novel: whilst Mrs Dashwood in 'Sense and Sensibility' is thought most unlikely to survive another fifteen years, although she is 'hardly forty'. We think of our Prime Minister as young at fifty-one, yet William Pitt the younger attained that office at the age of twenty-four.

We owe to Jung the idea that, about the age of thirty-seven, important changes tend to occur in most of us. His original realization of this was based on personal experience, for it was at this precise age that he himself went through a period of profound emotional disturbance which culminated in the publication of 'The Psychology of the Unconscious' and his break with Freud. It was at this time also, as a direct result of his own inner turmoil, that he advanced the initial formulation of the main psychological concepts which were to preoccupy him until his death in 1961.

One reason why early middle life is a critical point in development is that, at this age, many people lack any positive goal at which to aim. In adolescence, however disturbed this may be, the tasks facing a young person are crystal clear. A boy needs to establish his place in the pecking order, to gain what success his talents fit him for, and to prove himself as possessing courage and independence. A girl needs to found a home, to achieve the status of marriage, and to take the important step of changing from being a daughter to becoming a mother. Both sexes need to establish a confident sense of their admission to adult membership of their own sex.

By the late thirties many of these goals will have been achieved. Most people will have won a certain degree of emancipation from their parental background, and have achieved, if not autonomy, at least a measure of personal independence. Both sexes will have had experience of each other; and the majority will have married. A man will be established in his work; a woman have borne children; and, in the affluent society, a home will have been set up and immediate material needs fulfilled. It is just at this point that the old cliché of it being better to travel hopefully than to arrive becomes insistently valid.

It may seem paradoxical that, just when a human being has more or less mastered the difficulties of growing-up, and is at the height of his powers, life should present new problems. We cannot, however, maintain that the emotional upheavals which characterize this phase of life are the prerogative of a neurotic minority. Although the age group thirty to forty does not contain the majority of married people, the divorce rate is highest in this decade. The suicide rate is greater amongst the elderly: but the incidence of severe depression increases in the late thirties. Alcoholism may also become manifestly a problem at around the age of forty, probably, no doubt, because it is then that alcoholic addiction becomes increasingly a financial possibility. The less obviously disturbed often display a restless dissatisfaction which shows itself in transient infidelities, changes of occupation, or increasing moodiness and irritability.

It is often stated that the emotional disturbances of early middle age are the result of a decline in sexual potency and an increased awareness of the approach of death. But, as Kinsey has demonstrated, diminution in sexual performance is very gradual in men; whilst women often experience an increase in desire when pregnancy is no longer so likely. Nor, at the age of forty, is death a proximate threat, now that so many survive into extreme old age.

It is true that some of the depression which afflicts people in this age group is due to disappointment: for this is the age when men face the reality of their achievement and compare it, perhaps unfavourably, with the day-dreams of their youth. But it seems unlikely that this fact alone is enough to account for the symptoms of a disorder which is so widespread and which is even more prone to attack the successful than to afflict the less obviously fortunate.

Is it some secret, masochistic desire which drives people to make their lives unnecessarily complicated and difficult? At the beginning of middle age men and women not infrequently change their careers, their marriage partners and, less often, their whole way of life. Since the new career may be no more rewarding than the old, and the latter partner often closely resembles the former, it is tempting to explain such changes in terms of some deep-seated wish for punishment.

But the phenomena we are discussing are too common to be attributed to a need which is pathological; and the masochistic explanation, like the others discussed above, must be rejected as insufficient.

Over the past twenty years our views of instinct have changed. Before this, again influenced by Freud, we have tended to regard man as a creature whose invariable goal is a peaceful equilibrium. Sexual and aggressive tensions have been thought of as irritants to be got rid of; and sinking back into Boeotian bliss, satisfied, contented and at peace as the chief aim of man's existence.

In recent years we have come to realize that such a concept is insufficient. Not all animals who have their nutritional and sexual needs assuaged stay contentedly at rest. Even when replete with food and sensually satiated, rats, for example, become restless and show exploratory appetitive behaviour which demonstrates a desire to seek out new stimuli. The concept of all behaviour as being motivated by the need to reduce the tension caused by instinctive drives is overdue for revision. Recent research on the behaviour and mental capacities of men in isolation has shown that constantly changing stimulation is essential if normal functions are to be preserved. The human brain is an organ which works best in an environment which provides the stimulus of constant novelty.

In other words, it looks as if problems are a vital part of living, and that if no problems exist it is necessary for us to invent them. Man, unless he is to drown in a pool of stagnant discontent, seems to be a creature who can never rest upon his laurels but must always seek out new stimuli and discover new difficulties to surmount.

Some such concept might usefully explain the fact that it is just when the primary goals of his first half of life have been attained that the disturbances discussed here become so frequent. The need to set oneself new problems and the fact that development does not necessarily cease in middle life are amply demonstrated in the lives of the creatively gifted.

It is true that both mathematical invention and the gift of lyric poetry tend to die an early death; but other forms of creativity may flourish and deepen from middle age onwards to the furthest extreme of human existence. Verdi, composing 'Falstaff' at 80, and Titian, painting in extreme old age, are exceptional even among their peers: but most artists who have survived to continue working beyond the age of forty demonstrate in their compositions a preoccupation with new problems and changes of style which may often be reflected in their lives. It was not until the age of 38 that Ibsen achieved success with 'Brand', and it was at the same time that his manner, appearance and even his handwriting underwent a complete change. Moreover, a number of the creative do not discover their true paths until half of life has passed. George Eliot, for example, did not turn to fiction until she was nearly forty. Freud did not publish 'Studies in Hysteria' until he was thirty-nine; while 'The Interpretation of Dreams,' the work which he continued to regard as embodying his greatest creative insight, first appeared in 1899 when he was already forty-three.

It may be argued that what applies to the exceptional is untrue of the less gifted. In reality, however, the problems of human beings are perennial and similar. 'The troubles of our proud and angry dust are from eternity, and shall not fail.' The creative are not distinguished so much by an absence or an excess of the same difficulties which afflict us all as by their ability to make these manifest in their work, and thus render them more obvious.

It is possible that we are now moving into an era when, as Alex Comfort has suggested, the years around forty may be regarded as a second adolescence; a springboard for new departures and new interests rather than a plateau before descent. If so, we shall have to make more provision in society for men and women to make the changes they need. It has been suggested that we ought to have schools for forty-year-olds, to fit them for the second half of life, though in a society where it is impossible to get enough teachers for youth this is an Utopian idea. Yet it should be possible to reassess the abilities and potentialities of men and women at this age and to create a society in which greater flexibility allow more fulfilment in both work and creative recreation.

There are many people who, at the threshold of middle age, are more fully aware than they have ever been of both their strengths and their weaknesses, and would thus be better able to choose the type of work for which they were suited if only a choice were open to them. Similarly, there are a number of people who, when their children are grown up, would like to be free to find new possibilities of sexual happiness in the light of mature experience. Second marriages may even become the rule rather than the exception.

Whatever solutions society may ultimately approve, the fact remains that this second adolescent period is not one in which regret for the past need be a main feature, unless it be in the case of those unfortunates whose self-esteem is totally linked with physical prowess. Rather is it an age at which men and women can affirm their individual identities and look forward to new and enriching possibilities of future development.

Personality in later middle age

Felix Post

Dr Felix Post qualified in 1939 and has been a Consultant Psychiatrist at the Bethlem Royal Hospital and the Maudsley Hospital since 1947.

He has a special interest in problems of the elderly, on which he has published several papers and books.

As people become aware that they have entered middle age, they tend to become understandably concerned with the future – not hopefully expectant, but with some apprehension or even anxiety. In fact, a person may be said to have reached middle age only when he or she has become aware of a sense of finality: he realizes that he is not likely to get any further; time may bring with it certain promotions or increase in status, but by and large his course seems mapped out, and the time for retirement draws slowly but surely closer and closer. In this situation, there is little point in preaching resignation or in recommending programmes of preparation for old age. One simply cannot tell other people how to run their lives. It should, however, be possible to impart some factual information on personality changes due to ageing. Forewarned is forearmed.

Our prevailing intellectual climate favours an attitude which stresses environmental factors in shaping personality. It would be silly to deny that much good has come from our increasing awareness of early childhood influences, of the importance of good mothering, of the deleterious effects of parental disunity or of the father's inefficacy, and of the tremendous amount of thought which is being given to education. All the same, abnormal personalities may develop under most favourable circumstances, and on the other hand well adjusted and emotionally successful people often come from unfortunate backgrounds. In other words, a child who is favourably endowed genetically will withstand environmental stresses, which may permanently warp the mental and emotional growth of a child who has inherited personality weaknesses or deviations from the very persons who shape his early environment. From childhood onwards, we largely create our own environment, confining this term to the kind of persons we single out for interaction. Under civilized conditions the material environment is probably of subsidiary psychological importance. The choice of close associates, of the adolescent group, of friends made at work, and, most important, of sexual partners is, however, strongly influenced by inclinations formed in early childhood, mainly in relation to closely connected adult persons. To give but one example, there is a strong impression that the daughters of aggressive alcoholics choose similar husbands. Our individually unique habitual ways of experiencing, thinking, and behaving (and this is as good a definition of 'personality' as any) are thus shaped from childhood onwards by what is called out from us by others. To complete the circle, these others are chosen by us, because they seem to promise what are essentially repetitions of childhood relationships. The human environment selected in this way will, therefore, tend to reinforce personality characteristics laid down in early life, and these are compounded of hereditary-genetic factors and earliest childhood experiences.

The question as to which is more potent, nature or nurture, remains an open one, but the point of departure of our present discussion will be that the essential features of every individual personality are shaped in childhood and that life experiences will be utilized largely to the extent to which they fit the pattern laid down at that time. To put it concretely, a person with a friendly and trusting disposition will not be turned into a morose misanthrope through being occasionally let down or cheated by others, but a sensitive boy or girl who views the environment as largely hostile will seize upon experiences of this sort as confirming him in this attitude, and he is likely to become an increasingly aloof and suspicious person. Here we have the basis of an observation made since the earliest days of world literature: that with rising age, and especially in old age, certain personality traits are thrown more sharply into relief, that they are in fact *caricatured*.

It may then be helpful for the middle-aged person to realize the following: The way and the extent to which experiences in store for him during his later years are likely to alter his outlook and his attitudes will to a very large extent depend on the strengths and weaknesses of his adult personality. The moving away of children, retirement, loss of spouse through death, the threat to one's own life through sudden illness or through chronic disease and disabilities – all these are obviously severe crises, but they need not permanently interfere with a general sense that life remains definitely worthwhile. Investigations have shown that fear of approaching death diminishes considerably with increasing age in the average person. Though our present rules for compulsory retirement may be rather too rigid and unimaginative, dispassionately conducted studies agree in showing that, after some initial anxiety, physical and mental health tend to improve following retirement.

While it is suggested that stresses from the environment and from within, which are unavoidable during late life, will alter personality mainly by making weaknesses more apparent, the extent to which personality structure is changed by the ageing process must not be concealed. It is hoped to show, however, that these changes are appropriate and beneficial. Adopting a Darwinist outlook, we would agree that all organisms at present existing on this earth are optimally adapted to their living sphere. Since industrialization, and more recently since the communications explosion, the human environment has altered greatly from that obtaining for many preceding millennia. We shall briefly look at its possible effects on personality at a later stage. For the present, we shall accept that by means of the process of evolution homo sapiens has emerged as singularly well adapted. Leaving out many obvious other features, man is distinguished from all other species by surviving, not exceptionally, but in large numbers, beyond the reproductive period of life. In the case of all other animals, the survival of a species in competition with others was achieved by obtaining more adequate food supplies and through more profuse reproduction. In animals, life usually ends with reproductive capacity. Ageing changes affect muscles (of the heart as well as of the limbs), structures surrounding joints, visual acuity – to mention only a few. The less efficient individual, no longer useful to his species, will thus sooner or later fall victim to a predator or perish as a result of increasing malnutrition. Why is it that even in biblical times man was expected to live three score years or more, and that with the rise of civilization this expectation became increasingly the rule?

The answer is that man has remained useful for the survival of his species, or viewed more narrowly for that of his band or tribe, at a time when he is no longer able to increase its numbers. This continued usefulness is due to the evolution of language. Many animals are known to communicate by sound, but even in primates sounds are very largely used for signalling emotion. Man alone possesses propositional speech. He is able to store information not just within a system of reflexes, but in symbolic form (thoughts and words), and to communicate this stored information to others by speech. There is no need to expound in detail the ways in which at various stages of human development individuals in the post-reproductive period of life tended to play increasingly important roles as heads of families or as councils of the elders in larger communities. More closely related to our inquiry will be to demonstrate changes with age in personality structure which are optimally adapted to the role of the elderly in society.

The brain as the organ of the mind, together with certain closely associated endocrine glands, is responsible for all personality functions. Less well appreciated is that the many million cells (neurones) of the central nervous system are in contrast to many other types of body-cell irreplaceable: they no longer divide and multiply. Throughout childhood, brain function improves as increasing numbers of connections between nerve cells develop, and during adolescence brain function is at the height of its efficiency in terms of the level of excitation in the brain cells, the speed with which signals are transmitted, and the duration of reverberation among assemblies of cells. The learning of all skills is thus facilitated. These skills are first those of walking, talking, and those in-involved in simple manipulations; later comes the handling of symbols during primary, secondary, and higher education, or apprenticeship.

Intellectual changes with ageing are more expertly described in a later article in this book. Here we shall only point out that probably due to changes of intracellular protein structure neurones gradually become less efficient. As a result, thought and action become slower, and on account of impaired short term storage of information, learning of new facts and new skills becomes more difficult. Learning remains possible throughout life, but it is more laborious, requiring more frequent repetitions and a larger number of intermediate stages. Returning to our Darwinian model, this does not present any real handicap for adaptation. In any species, the adult organism in comparison with the developing individual can get by very well without much new learning. In man, the need for new learning throughout adult life persists, but it usually affects only a few areas of adjustment, and in contrast with childhood there is plenty of time for learning to take place. Much more of a handicap is that ageing affects not only the efficiency of the short term storage mechanisms necessary for learning, but also functions which subserve the retention of things remembered, and the ability to reproduce from long term storage facts, figures, faces, names or events. It is well known that with advancing age, recent matters are often poorly recalled, and that one has increasing recourse to various mnemotechnical devices. This decline of memory function, especially for things that matter little, is an imperceptibly gradual one. Rapid and devastating declines occur in arterio-sclerotic and senile brain deteriorations (dementias), which occur with increasing frequency after the age of seventy, but even then only in a quite small proportion of persons.

Many personality changes with ageing, which are not in the intellectual sphere, can be traced to increasing difficulties in acquiring new skills and abilities, to decreasing capacity of learning, as well as to mental slowing. In performing tasks, older persons tend to use time-saving devices, involving the employment of routines; older people thus are inclined to be more methodical and tidy than younger ones; they tend to deviate less from essentials. On the debit side, they also avoid situations of new learning, are thus less adaptable, more rigid, and more conservative in attitude. They are less open to new concepts and inspiration. For this reason scientists, mathematicians, and artists produce their best work in their twenties and thirties. Vocations demanding integration of slowly accumulating knowledge like the law and medicine are associated with the greatest achievements more often at later ages. There are many exceptions, and creative minds frequently operate well into the senile period of life, producing outstandingly beautiful distillates of human experience, such as Verdi's 'Falstaff', and the closing scenes of 'Faust', a dramatic poem which occupied Goethe on and off throughout a long and increasingly rich life. We average mortals remain indefinitely capable of following our customary pursuits, or similar ones after retirement. Our limits are usually set not by mental decline, but by physical troubles.

The most primitive form of learning occurs by imitation, but all learning depends on being able to receive communications from the outside, and a strongly outward directed attitude (extroversion) is essential for learning to occur. In parallel with an agewise decline in learning ability, the extroverted attitude gradually shifts towards increasing introversion. The young tend to move in crowds, while numerous investigations have confirmed that older persons prefer activities carried out alone or with only one or two other persons. The lengths to which this inward turning may go depend on the original personality, culture, and perhaps social class.

But under all circumstances, there seems to be a tendency for young adults to move outside their families, while the elderly are predominantly family centred. Awareness of one's body is outward directed in youth. Physical display aims at attracting others towards the achievement of the most intimate of all communications in sexual relationship. Waning sexual libido may thus be another cause of decreasing extroversion with age, especially operating in the later years. Bodily interests tend to be turned inward, literally: preoccupations with the inner workings of the body, especially of the bowels, which have been shown to increase with age. In psychoanalytic terms, there is thus a libidinal shift from genital to anal levels, from giving to retaining. In the highest age ranges, the shift from extroversion towards introversion may lead to emotional disengagement. Deeply felt interests are withdrawn from the environment. Relationships tend to be increasingly valued to the extent to which they satisfy simple personal needs. Beyond this, identification with others becomes more shallow or tends to cease altogether.

Looked at from the standpoint of a young adult, all the changes due to ageing which we have sketched out, clearly present a long catalogue of declines and deteriorations. It is claimed, however, that these changes due to psycho-motor slowing, impaired memory and learning ability, decline in sexual drive, as well as shift of libidinal organization make for optimal adaptation of the ageing person in human society. Collective cultural traditions continue to be carried and transmitted by the elderly, at a humble level by the grandfather and the grandmother, at the highest by the teacher, administrator, or leader. At the same time, members of the older generation tend to withdraw increasingly from competition not just in the areas of economics, but also in that of interpersonal relationships. Obviously, this withdrawal and change of roles does not always gosmoothly: the father–son problem, the mother-in-law problem, the restriction of the elderly in modern Western society, are just a few examples.

At an individual level maladjustments may arise from the

fact that the ageing personality and the ageing brain are especially vulnerable, and apt to be impaired by disease in the widest sense of the word much more frequently and severely than in younger persons. Numerically far more important are minor personality disturbances, which alone shall concern us here. An emotionally stable person, not unduly given to introspection, optimistic, and pleasurably outward directed, is unlikely to become unhappy in old age, especially as he tends to be surrounded in his family by similar persons. His or her sexual adjustment in marriage has probably been satisfactory, and sexual relations tend to be continually satisfactory, until they gradually cease well after the age of seventy or later. Slight impairment of judgement and self-control may make such a person excessively possessive, domineering, and irascible. The ageing of persons with lifelong neurotic propensities and other signs of emotional maladjustment may prove more troublesome. Many of these disturbances may have been due to psychosexual difficulties, and certain neuroses tend to improve with increasing age probably because there is a decline of libidinal pressures. Aggressively outgoing behaviour which includes habitually delinquent conduct also tends to improve once late adolescence is passed. However, the timidly anxious, pessimistic, and excessively inward looking personality may fare badly, probably due to increasing further introversion with age. Anxieties over health often turn into hypochondriasis, anxieties over money into miserliness. A person who has always looked upon the outside world as largely hostile, may become frankly asocial, withdrawn, cantankerous, suspicious, or even given to persecutory interpretations. Undue tendencies towards pessimistic worrying and irrational anxieties are usually markedly increased in the elderly, and they rather than physical disabilities are the most frequent causes of restriction of activities, and of unwelcome overdependence on others. Unfortunately, middle and late life brings with it a host of experiences which are anxiety provoking: financial restriction, loss of children as they marry or move away, widowing, physical illness, pain, inability to leave the home, and an increasing awareness of the proximity of death. Most people come to terms with all these stresses astonishingly well, but those with lifelong proneness towards excessive anxiety often become a problem to themselves and to others.

Much evidence favours the view that the emotional upset caused by sudden and severe, or by long accumulated anxiety, may lead to the clinical condition of depression. In a mild form this is said to occur commonly in ageing people, perhaps in one of every four persons. A mood of sadness, loss of interest, poor sleep and appetite may last only a day or two, but may recur every few months. The more serious form of the dis-disorder is seen in very few people, though the frequency with which it shows itself increases with rising age. Depression is, therefore, the greatest single cause of mental illhealth between the ages of forty and seventy, and during these years there is also a steep rise of the suicide rate. In keeping with the finding that the great majority of sufferers had in the past been over anxious and excessively worrying people, the illness starts in a high proportion soon after a serious, or at any rate unaccustomed and to the sufferer threatening illness. Loss or merely the threatened loss of a loved person is the second commonest cause of depression from middle age onwards.

It cannot be overstressed that the great majority of ageing people change little, and for reasons given in the first part of this article, show excellent adaptation to the special demands and restriction of middle and late life. Is there any sign that the so-called stresses of modern life may disturb adjustment? It is difficult to interpret statistics collected over the last one hundred years, but there is very little evidence to suggest that there has been an increase of mental or nervous illhealth among the elderly. The greater strain on our mental health services is, of course, due to the increase in the number of persons 'at risk'. The elderly nowadays are more often than used to be forced to live on their own, but true isolation is infrequent. Their lives are enriched, even when they are housebound, by wireless and television. Deaf aids are effective and freely available. Physical illness is much more efficiently treated, and pain almost always considerably relieved.

Earlier on it was stated that one cannot advise people on how to run their lives and on how to grow old. It is hoped that the information given here may help towards the recognition of danger signals. Increasing self knowledge backed by more information now increasingly available may lead to personal reorientation and happier adjustment. Where breakdown threatens or has actually occurred medical and psychiatric action is nowadays highly successful in the great majority of cases. However, it still rests with the individual to recognize in time that outside help may be needed.

The awareness of middle age*

Bernice L. Neugarten

Professor Bernice L. Neugarten is on the Committee in Human Development at the University of Chicago. Her work has largely been of a socio-psychological character and in the last ten years she has been increasingly interested in the process of ageing. The work reported here is one of the very few studies in the world which have dealt specifically with middle age.

In a recent issue of *Time*, that widely-read magazine of news and editorial opinion that appears each week in United States, there appeared on the front cover a picture of Lauren Bacall, the movie actress, and the caption, 'The Command Generation.' The cover story turned out to be a journalist's description of middle age and of the position of the 40-to-60-year-old group in the current American scene. After the rueful recognition that, unhappily, Lauren Bacall is not an altogether typical representative of the age group – not, at least, on the basis of our own studies – the next appraisal was that the caption was not an inept one and that it reflected the same evaluation of middle age that has emerged in most of our own interviews with adults of various ages.[1]

* This study has been carried out in collaboration with Dr Ruth J. Kraines, Lecturer in Human Development, University of Chicago, and Dr James E. Birren, Professor of Psychology, University of Southern California. A full presentation of the data is now in preparation and is expected to appear soon in book form.

1 An extensive set of studies has been carried out in the Committee on Human Development at the University of Chicago over the past decade: studies of personality, of adaptational patterns, of career lines, of age-norms and age-appropriate behaviour in adults, and of attitudes and values across social-class and generational lines. The total number of men and women who have participated now totals something over 2,000. Each study in the series has been based upon a relatively large sample of normal people, none of them volunteers, and all of them residing in one or another metropolitan community in the middle west.

Middle-aged men and women, while they by no means regard themselves as being in command of all they survey, nevertheless recognize that they constitute the powerful age-group vis-à-vis other age groups; that they are the norm-bearers and the decision-makers; and they live in a society which, while it may be oriented towards youth, is controlled by the middle-aged. In this sense, the *Time* editors have a view that is consonant with our own, even if theirs has been less laboriously derived and more colourfully stated.

There is space here to describe only a few of the psychological issues of middle age as they have emerged from our studies; and to draw primarily from only one of our investigations, one in which 100 well-placed men and women were interviewed at length concerning the salient characteristics of middle adulthood. These people were selected randomly from a pool of names originally drawn from University alumni lists, various business and professional directories, with some drawn also from *American Men of Science* and *Who's Who in America*.

The enthusiasm manifested by these persons as the interviews progressed was only one of many confirmations that middle age is a period of heightened sensitivity to one's position within a complex social environment; and that reassessment of the self is a prevailing theme. Most of this group, as anticipated, were highly introspective and highly verbal persons who evidenced considerable insight into the changes that had taken place in their careers, their families, their status, and in the ways in which they dealt with both their inner and outer worlds. Generally the higher the individual's career position the greater was his willingness to explore the various issues and themes of middle age. In a sense these persons were employing their talents in mapping out for us the dimensions of their lives and in acting as highly-qualified informants about themselves and others whom they had observed.[2]

[2] The description of this sample is worth stressing, since all too often the attention of the psychologist has been focussed upon the problem

The delineation of middle age

There is ample evidence in our data that middle age is perceived as a distinctive period in the life cycle, one which is qualitatively different from other age periods. Chronological age is no longer the positive marker that it was earlier in life, when to become older means to become bigger, more attractive, or more important, neither is it the positive marker that it becomes again in advanced old age, when each additional year lived increased one's distinction. Middle-aged people look to their positions within different life contexts – body, career, family – rather than to chronological age for their primary cues in clocking themselves. Often there is a differential rhythm in the timing of events within these various contexts so that the cues utilized for placing oneself in this period of the life-cycle are not always synchronous. For example, one business executive regards himself as being on top in his occupation and assumes all the prerogatives that go with seniority in that context, yet, because his children are still young, he feels he has a long way to go before completing his major goals within the family.

Distance from the young

Generally the middle-ager sees himself as the bridge between the generations, both within the family and within the wider contexts of work and community. At the same time he has a clear sense of differentiation from both the younger and older generations. In his view, young people cannot understand nor relate to the middle-aged because they have not accumulated the perquisite life experiences. Both the particular historical events and the general accumulation of experience

---

cases or upon the clinical populations that present themselves for study, to the neglect of the normal or the highly successful. As yet we have no developmental psychology of adulthood; and psychology as a science has just begun to study the five or six decades that constitute the adult portion of the life span with something of the fascination that it has been studying the first two decades that constitute childhood and adolescence.

create generational identification and mark the boundaries between generations. One 48-year-old says,

> 'I graduated from college in the middle of the Great Depression. A degree in Sociology didn't prepare you for jobs that didn't exist, so I became a social worker because there were openings in that field . . . Everybody was having trouble eking out an existence, and it took all your time and energy . . . Today's young people are different. They've grown up in an age of affluence. When I was my son's age, I was much more worldly, what with the problems I had to face. I was supporting my father's family at his age. But my son can never understand all this . . . he's of a different generation altogether . . .'

The middle-ager becomes increasingly aware of the distance – emotionally, socially, and culturally – between himself and the young. Sometimes the awareness comes as a sudden revelation:

> 'I used to think that all of us in the office were contemporaries, for we all had similar career interests. But one day we were talking about old movies and we realized that the younger ones had never seen a Shirley Temple film or an Our Gang comedy . . . Then it struck me with a blow that I was older than they. I had never been so conscious of it before . . .'

Similarly, another man remarked:

> 'When I see a pretty girl on the stage or in the movies – we used to say 'a cute chick' – and when I realize, 'My God, she's about the age of my son', it's a real shock. It makes me realize that I'm middle-aged.'

An often-expressed preoccupation is how one should relate to both younger and older persons and how to act one's age. Most of our respondents are acutely aware of their responsibility to the younger generation and with what we called 'the creation of social as well as biological heirs.' One corporation executive says,

> 'I worry lest I no longer have the rapport with young people that I had some years back. I think the reason I'm becoming uncomfortable with them is that they're so uncomfortable with me. They treat me like I treated my own employer when I was 25. I was frightened of him . . . But one of my main problems now is to encourage young people to develop so that they'll be able to carry on after us . . .'

And a 50-year-old woman says,

> 'You always have younger people looking to you and asking questions . . . You don't want them to think you're a blubbering fool . . . You try to be adequate as a model . . .'

A newspaper writer, not himself one of our respondents, summarized the feelings of many of these men and women in the following words:

> '. . . the realization suddenly struck me that I had become, perhaps not an old fogy but surely a middle-aged fogy . . . For the train was filled with college boys returning from vacation . . . They cruised up and down the aisles, pretending to be tipsy . . . boisterous, but not obnoxious; looking for fun, but not for trouble . . . Yet most of the adult passengers were annoyed with them, including myself. I sat there, feeling a little like Eliot's Prufrock, "so meticulously composed, buttoned-up, bespectacled, mouth thinly set" . . . Squaresville.'

The awareness that one's parents' generation is now quite old does not lead to the same feeling of distance from the parental generation as from the younger generation.

> 'I sympathize with old people, now, in a way that is new. I watch my parents, for instance, and I wonder if I will age in the same way.'

The sense of proximity and identification with the old is enhanced by the feeling that those who are older are in a position to understand and appreciate the responsibilities and commitments to which the middle-aged have fallen heir.

> 'My parents, even though they are much older, can understand what we are going through; just as I now understand what they went through . . .'

Although the idiosyncrasies of the aged may be annoying to the middle-aged, an effort is usually made to keep such feelings under control. There is greater projection of the self in one's behaviour with older people, sometimes to the extent of blurring the differences between the two generations. One of our women recounted an incident that betrayed her apparent lack of awareness (or denial) of her mother's ageing:

> 'I was shopping with mother. She had left something behind on the counter and the clerk called out to tell me that the 'old lady' had forgotten her package. I was amazed. Of course the clerk was a young man and she must have seemed old to him. But the interesting thing is that I myself don't think of her as old . . . She doesn't seem old to me . . .'

Differences between men and women

Women, but not men, tend to define their age status in terms of timing of events within the family cycle. For married women, middle age is closely tied to the launching of children into the adult world, and even unmarried career women often discuss middle age in terms of the family they might have had. One single woman said,

> 'Well, fifteen years ago I didn't consider myself middle-aged. Before I was thirty-five, the future just stretched forth, far away . . . I think I am doing now what I want. In fact, the things that troubled me in my thirties about marriage and children don't bother me now because I'm at the age where many women have already lost their husbands . . . I have

two nieces and three nephews, and I enjoy them very much without having any of the worries and burdens that go with it.'

Men, on the other hand, perceive the onset of middle age by cues presented outside the family context, often from the deferential behaviour accorded them in the work setting. One man described the first time a younger associate held open a door for him; another, being called by his official title by a newcomer in the company; another, the first time he was ceremoniously asked for advice by a younger man.

Men perceive a close relationship between life-line and career-line. Middle age is the time to take stock. Any disparity noted between career-expectations and career achievements – that is, whether one is 'on time' or 'late' in reaching career goals – adds to the heightened awareness of age. One 47-year-old lawyer said,

> 'I moved at age forty-five from a large corporation to a law firm. I got out at the last possible moment, because after forty-five it is too difficult to find the job you want. If you haven't made it by then, you had better make it fast, or you are stuck.'

The most dramatic cues for the male, however, are often biological. The increased attention centred upon his health; the decrease in the efficiency of the body; the death of friends of the same age – these are the signs that prompt many men to describe bodily changes as the most salient characteristic of middle age.

> 'Mentally I still feel young, but suddenly one day my son beat me at tennis . . .'

Or,

> 'It was the sudden heart attack in a friend that made the difference. I realized that I could no longer count on my body as I used to do . . .'

Health changes are more of an age marker for men than for women. Despite the menopause and other manifestations of the climacterium – an event, incidentally, to which very few of these women attach psychological significance – women refer much less frequently to biological changes and to concern over health. 'Body-monitoring' is the term we used to describe the large variety of protective strategies for maintaining the middle-aged body at given levels of performance and appearance; but while these issues take the form of a new sense of physical vulnerability in men, they take the form of a 'rehearsal for widowhood' in women. Women are more concerned over the body-monitoring of their husbands than of themselves.

Another difference between the sexes is marked. Most of the women interviewed feel that the most conspicuous characteristic of middle age is the sense of increased freedom. Not only is there increased time and energy now available for the self, but also a satisfying change in self-concept. Whether married or single, the typical theme is that middle age marks the beginning of a period in which latent talents and capacities can be put to use in new directions.

Some of these women describe this sense of freedom coming at the same time that their husbands are reporting increased job pressures or – something equally troublesome – job boredom. Contrast this typical statement of a woman,

> 'I discovered these last few years that I was old enough to admit to myself the things I could do well and to start doing them. I didn't think like this before . . . It's a great new feeling . . .'

with the statement of one man,

> 'You're thankful your health is such that you can continue working up to this point. It's a matter of concern to me right now because I'm forty-seven, and I have two children in college to support . . .'

or with the statement of another man, this one a history professor,

> 'I'm afraid I'm a bit envious of my wife. She went to work a few years ago, when our children no longer needed her attention, and a whole new world has opened to her. But myself? I just look forward to writing another volume, and then another volume . . .'

The changing time-perspective

Both sexes, although men more than women, talked of the new difference in the way time is perceived. Life is restructured in terms of time-left-to-live rather than time-since-birth. Not only the reversal in directionality, but the awareness that time is finite, is a particularly conspicuous feature of middle age. Thus,

> 'You hear so much about deaths that seem premature. That's one of the changes that comes over you over the years. Young fellows never give it a thought . . .'

The recognition that there is 'only so much time left' was a frequent theme in the interviews. In referring to the death of a contemporary, one man said,

> 'There is now the realization that death is very real. Those things don't quite penetrate when you're in your twenties and you think that life is all ahead of you. Now you know that death will come to you, too.'

Another said,

> 'Time is now a two-edged sword. To some of my friends, it acts as a prod; to others, a brake. It adds a certain anxiety, but I must also say it adds a certain zest in seeing how much pleasure can still be obtained, how many good years one can still arrange, how many new activities can be undertaken . . .'

The prime of life

Despite the new realization of the finiteness of time, one of the most prevailing themes expressed by these middle-aged respondents is that middle adulthood is the period of maximum capacity and ability to handle a highly complex environment and a highly differentiated self. Very few express a wish to be young again. As one of them said,

> 'There is a difference between wanting to *feel* young and wanting to *be* young. Of course it would be pleasant to maintain the vigour and appearance of youth; but I would not trade those things for the authority or the autonomy I feel – no, nor the ease of interpersonal relationships nor the self-confidence that comes from experience.'

The middle-aged individual, having learned to cope with the many contingencies of childhood, adolescence and young adulthood, now has available to him a substantial repertoire of strategies for dealing with life. One woman put it,

> 'I know what will work in most situations, and what will not. I am well beyond the trial and error stage of youth. I now have a set of guidelines . . . And I am practised . . .'

Whether or not they are correct in their assessments, most of our respondents perceive striking improvement in their exercise of judgement. For both men and women, the perception of greater maturity and a better grasp of realities is one of the most reassuring aspects of being middle-aged.

> 'You feel you have lived long enough to have learned a few things that nobody can learn earlier. That's the reward . . . and also the excitement. I now see things in books, in people, in music that I couldn't see when I was younger . . . It's a form of ripening that I attribute largely to my present age . . .'

A vice-president of a large publishing company said,

> 'When I think back over the errors I made when I was 28 or 30 or 35, I am amazed at the young men today who think they can take over their companies at 28. They can't possibly have the maturity required . . . True maturity doesn't come until around 45 . . . And while some of the young men are excellently educated, we middle-aged men are no longer learning from a book. We've learned from past experience . . .'

There are a number of manifestations of this sense of competence. There is, for instance, the 45-year-old's sensitivity to the self as the instrument by which to reach his goals; what we have called a preoccupation with self-utilization (as contrasted to the self-consciousness of the adolescent):

> 'I know now exactly what I can do best, and how to make the best use of my time . . . I know how to delegate authority, but also what decisions to make myself . . . I know how to buffer myself from troublesome people . . . one well-placed telephone call will get me what I need. It takes time to learn how to cut through the red tape and how to get the organization to work for me . . . All this is what makes the difference between me and a young man, and it's all this that gives me the advantage . . .'

There is the heightened self-understanding that provides gratification. One perceptive woman described it in these terms:

> 'It is as if there are two mirrors before me, each held at a partial angle. I see part of myself in my mother who is growing old, and part of her in me. In the other mirror, I see part of myself in my daughter. I have had some dramatic insights, just from looking in those mirrors . . . It is a set of relevations that I suppose can only come when you are in the middle of three generations.'

There is also the keen sense of expertise. One man said,

> 'I believe in making decisions . . . They may appear to others to be snap decisions, for I make them quickly and I don't look back and worry about what might have been if it had been done another way. I've had enough experience . . . I've been through it fifty times, so when I make decisions that seem to come out of the clear blue sky, they just represent a big lot of experience. I've been over the same ground before and I have the ready answer . . .'

In pondering the data on these men and women, we have been impressed with the central importance of what might be called the executive processes of personality in middle age: self-awareness, selectivity, manipulation and control of the environment, mastery, competence, the wide array of cognitive strategies.

We are impressed, too, with reflection as a striking characteristic of the mental life of middle-aged persons: the stocktaking, the heightened introspection, and above all, the structuring and restructuring of experience – that is, the conscious processing of new information in the light of what one has already learned; and turning one's proficiency to the achievement of desired ends.

These people feel that they effectively manipulate their social environments on the basis of prestige and expertise; and that they create many of their own rules and norms. There is a sense of increased control over impulse life. The successful middle-aged person often describes himself as no longer 'driven', but as now the 'driver' – in short, 'in command'.

PART 2 THE BODY

Health hazards: 1 The size and nature of the risks

Dr R. F. L. Logan, M.D., M.R.C.P., D.I.H.

Dr Robert F. L. Logan was born in 1917, in Bangor, N. Ireland. Having graduated from Queen's University, Belfast and qualified as a doctor he went to sea for three years, returning in 1945 to Manchester as Nuffield Fellow of Industrial Medicine. Since 1959 he has been Director of the Medical Care Research Unit in Manchester.

Middle age is the stage of life which seems to recede as the individual himself becomes older. In U.S.A. with its virile worship of youthfulness, adolescence is deemed to persist into the sixties and to admit to middle age is to be an unpopular and deviant failure. As the label is so charged with emotion, here in Britain we will say it is the 'prime' of life and it lies in the middle between the climacteric and the onset of senescence. It may be split for artificial statistical analysis into two decades – ages 45–54 as early middle age and 55–64 as late middle age. The hazards to living will be considered first as the risk of dying, then admission to hospital, surgery, calling in the family doctor and being absent from work due to sickness.

1. Death Rates: an international comparison

With the explosion of clinical discoveries in the 1940s and 1950s, sickness became less hazardous and so there was a sharp fall in most death rates and at most ages. The benefits of antibiotics were highest in infancy and childhood where the sulfonamides and penicillin saved the lives of children with such infections as those of the bowel, brain and lungs like pneumonia. In middle age the benefits were less miraculous except with tuberculosis where chemotherapy conquered the white plague and obsolescent sanitoria have been converted now into geriatric hospitals. After the initial impact of these wonder drugs in the '40's and '50's the returns are naturally diminishing. The improvements have now largely worked themselves out so that there has been a deceleration in the falling death rates and indeed, those in middle and later life have tended to flatten out and remain static (Table I). By the very nature of disease today, non-infectious and 'degenerative', chronic or relapsing, with a complex mesh of causes interacting between inheritance and ways of living, affluence and personal habits, any hope of control by a breakthrough on a single link is unreal, and a different strategy (or a jungle campaign) is required in containing the hazards to health today. For the same reasons it is unlikely that those in middle age today can hope for much, if any, improvements in risks of death or sickness in their lifetime.

I Death rates per 1,000 middle-aged in recent decades in England and Wales

Year	*Male* 45–54	55–64	*Female* 45–54	55–64
1931	11·6	23·9	8·3	17·6
1951	8·6	24·3	5·3	13·0
1961	7·3	21·9	4·5	10·8
1965	7·4	21·4	4·4	10·3

Following the successful conquest of infection, the captains of death in middle age to be faced today have been reduced to a dominant two. Cancer and heart disease account for *thirty per cent* each of all deaths. The corporals of death add another ten per cent for the arterial catastrophes of strokes and seven per cent for bronchitis in England. Thus cancer and arterial disease together account for *seventy per cent* of all deaths and apart from these two big hazards, middle age is safe. Indeed, it is the safest age for violent deaths including suicide and motor traffic. These rank fourth at four per cent because all the other risks are so small (Fig. 1 and Table VII).

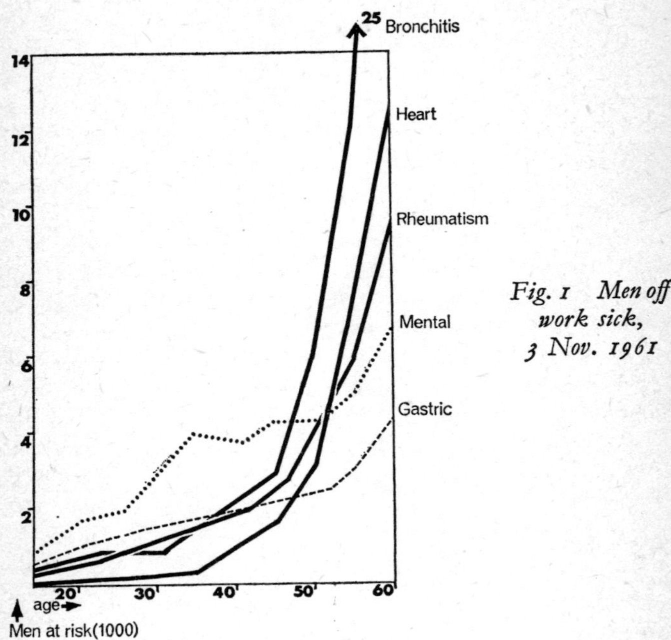

Fig. 1 Men off work sick, 3 Nov. 1961

The benefits of chemotherapy and modern surgery are no longer restricted to the developed countries of North America and Europe. Brinkmanship is successful in middle age in South America and the developing countries so that this pattern of death is now international and only alters after these front rankers, with local national killers.

The English killing disease is, of course, chronic bronchitis accounting for seven per cent even in middle age, but our drinking habits have spared us so far the fatal alcoholic livers of other over-developed or over-indulgent countries (Table II).

II Cirrhosis of liver

Rank in cause of death 1960 age 45–64

	New York	California	France	Italy	Sweden	England & Wales
Male	3	3	5	6	7	20+
Female	4	4	4	4	8	10+

Although the leading causes of death hold the same rank across all developed countries, the middle-aged die at different rates from the same diseases in each country and these add up to considerable differences in risk of death. Britain is far from the top in the world league of a score of developed countries and, in the European competition, is nearer to the bottom. Middle-aged men in Sweden die at almost half the rate of those in Scotland (Table III). Neither do the chances improve for those who reach retirement. Indeed, by the time men and women have passed their prime of life, their chances of survival from 65 to 85 for men in Norway are double those in England, and the gap has not narrowed in recent years – and France is improving its lead on us. (Table IV). Out of every 1,000 men age 65, 262 in Norway will survive to their eighty-fifth birthday but only 139 in England. Amongst women, the Norwegians again have the brightest prospects of survival, but the differences internationally are less for women than for men, and indeed the English woman is catching up with the brighter prospects of her overseas sisters. Out of every 1,000 women age 65, 321 in Norway will celebrate her eighty-fifth birthday while 284 in England can hope to do so. However, this enhancement of her survival makes her even more likely to be a widow while her English husband

III Death rates per 1,000 in middle age in some developed countries in 1963

MEN

Ages	45–49	50–54	55–59	60–64
Sweden	4·0	6·2	10·9	18·8
Holland	4·4	7·5	12·8	20·6
Canada	5·7	9·4	15·4	24·1
Italy	5·8	9·3	15·5	25·0
England and Wales	5·4	9·5	17·1	28·8
Scotland	7·2	11·9	21·0	34·0

WOMEN

Ages	45–49	50–54	55–59	60–64
Sweden	2·9	4·1	6·7	10·7
Holland	2·7	4·1	6·2	10·5
Canada	3·3	5·1	7·9	13·2
Italy	3·4	5·1	7·8	12·8
England and Wales	3·6	5·3	8·3	13·7
Scotland	4·4	6·6	10·3	17·4

is marking time. Indeed, it is men in late middle age who are the only male group to mark time in risk of dying, whilst their women folk continue to improve so that the gap has widened and for the past decade men aged 55–64 have been dying at twice the rate of their female peers. When these different chances of survival are translated into expectations of life in middle age, it is seen (Table V) that all age groups of women continue to extend their lead over men whose life expectancy only improved from up to 1950, but has been static since and, if anything, there is a grim suggestion of a decline.

In the early 1930's women aged 35 could expect another 37 years of life and the clinical advances of the 1940's and 1950's extended this by four more years to 41 years. The advance for men of the same age was only an added expectation of life from 34 to 36 years. At age 55 women's expectation advanced from 20 years in 1930 to 23 years in 1963; but for men, the expectation of surviving until 85 has stood still across the past three decades, at 18 years for those aged 55, and 12 years for those aged 65. Indeed, since 1948 the expectation of life in men from 35 onwards has not changed.

IV Chances of surviving from 65 to 85 (per 1,000)

	Men		*Women*	
	1950	1962	1950	1962
Norway	263	262	300	321
Holland	231	235	255	286
Canada	205	222	275	332
Sweden	204	216	233	287
U.S.A. (White)	189	201	278	334
France	136	170	242	302
England and Wales	132	139	235	284

V Expectation of life in England and Wales

Age	*Males*			*Females*		
	1930–2	1948–50	1963	1930–2	1948–50	1963
35	33·9	36·0	36·1	36·9	40·1	41·3
45	25·5	27·0	26·8	28·3	30·9	31·9
55	17·9	18·8	18·5	20·2	22·4	23·1
65	11·3	12·3	11·8	13·1	14·6	15·1

Within England and Wales there is a steady increase in death rates as one leaves the prosperous conditions of the

South and the Eastern Counties and proceeds to the industrial conurbations of the Midlands and the North. Here, heavy industry in Lancashire and the North-East has a legacy of slums and over-crowding, air pollution from factory chimneys, and more families in the labouring class than in the new clean and light industries with semi-skilled workers in the developing South. Moreover, since the unemployment of the hungry thirties, there has been a steady drift south, and perhaps it was the fitter workers who migrated, thus leaving behind the sick and the handicapped. Such complex social reasons must be behind the bare statistics that middle-aged men and women in the northern industrial towns died at up to 140 per cent of the rate of the Eastern Counties (Table VI). Their diseases are the same as in other countries, as are the better prospects for the women over their menfolk.

VI Death rates in middle and later life

Conurbations	*Age 45–64* M.	F.
Mersey	17	8
S.E. Lancs	17	8
Tyne	17	8
West Yorks	16	8
West Midlands	15	7
London	13	7
England and Wales	14	7
Eastern counties	12	6

2. *The killer diseases*

The reasons for this, of course, lie in the nature of the killing diseases (Table VII) with the men succumbing to ischemic heart diseases, lung cancer and bronchitis at over five times the rate of women and from road accidents, suicides and other violent deaths at twice the female rate.

VII Leading causes of death in middle age in England and Wales 1965 (per million)

	Males		*Females*	
	45–54	55–64	45–54	55–64
Coronary heart	2435	6800	391	1794
Other cardio vascular	578	1796	481	1257
Strokes	460	1740	388	1334
All cancer	2040	6115	1998	3640
Bronchitis	351	1824	97	315
Pneumonia	148	519	100	293
Suicide	185	256	141	180
Motor traffic	175	222	68	106
Other violent death	200	279	75	132
All other causes	791	1885	618	1274
Total deaths	7363	21436	4357	10325

Personal air pollution from cigarette smoking is the common and dominant factor in this self destruction, from coronary catastrophe, lung cancer and bronchitis. The successes in controlling infections like tuberculosis and pneumonia have been more than redressed in men by the steady climb in deaths from coronary heart disease and lung cancer. Women as a regiment are not yet smoking as much as the trousered male and, whilst they are still menstruating, have some biochemical protection from their hormones against coronary artery disease. It is these two assets that enable them to continue to draw ahead in life's stakes.

CORONARY HEART DISEASE

The dominant modern epidemic is ischemic heart disease and, because it seems to strike out of the blue and often fatally, generates as much fantasy about its causes as fear in the minds of the man, his wife and his doctor. From 1930 this new epidemic doubled its death toll each decade, and has now risen to such dimensions that twenty per cent of all middle-aged men can expect to develop clinical ischemic heart disease during middle life. With such feelings of helplessness there is a natural urge to grasp at any hope (such as anticoagulants). It is only now that some untangling of the inter-related mesh of factors lying in the background of inheritance, experience and mode of life is becoming clear. However, as in all disease today, some groups of folk carry a higher risk than their more fortunate fellow men. In the high risk group, one in six men can expect an attack within five years of early middle age and in later years it may increase to become one in three over the whole span of middle age. At the same time the more fortunate low risk men have only one-twelfth the risk with one in seventy-five expecting an attack in five years of middle age.

The outstanding work of Professor J. N. Morris and his team of epidemiologists over the past twenty years on the prevalence in different occupations showed the importance of physical exercise. On the double deck buses in London the conductors get about half as many heart attacks as the drivers and fewer of their attacks are immediately fatal. The conductor is also slimmer and puts on less weight than the sedentary driver. Similarly, the postman on his rounds is protected by his exercise compared with his colleague behind the counter or in the office.

These findings suggest some clues to the rise in this modern epidemic from the small levels of heart trouble such as angina suffered by our grandfathers – but not until their sixties. It is probable that the heavy physical toil of their labouring at work developed the blood supply to the muscles of their hearts as well as their brawny arms. Food was not as plentiful as today and cigarette smoking not a national addiction. Even to get to the place of work for the well-to-do needed some exercise – and thick soles on their boots in contrast to the wafer-thin shoes of today. Indeed their thighs and calves would not fit into the narrow trousers of today. Their health problems were those related to poverty, slums, sweat and toil and under-feeding. Our problems are those of affluence, over-smoking, over-eating and obesity whilst electric power has replaced human muscle. Indeed on an average Saturday or Sunday Professor Morris found that the only exercise taken by the average executive class civil servant was about one hour gardening, a second hour on household chores, a third hour on do-it-yourself tasks and another three hours on mild 'miscellaneous activities'. Bank clerks similarly rested and enjoyed *la dolce vita* with 'all mod. con.' and then drove by car to work.

Disease, of course, is the outcome of the interaction of the external environment and national mode of living today, with increased leisure and sedentary jobs, with the personal habits of over-smoking and over-eating of the individual in the family, and with his own biochemical inheritance of susceptibility to particular diseases. For example, difficulties in coping with a high sugar intake are inherited and may manifest themselves as diabetes. However, recent studies suggest that before the stage of requiring treatment such as insulin for the diabetes, the arteries such as the coronary to the heart muscle are affected and liable to thrombosis. Again, the early stages of increase in blood pressure are also associated with coronary heart disease. The short tubby man with a family history of diabetes, or stroke at any age, or sudden death before age sixty, with a generous roll of fat around his waist, size seventeen collar, successful but anxious about a date-line, this is the caricature of the potential candidate.

A picture can be drawn of the annual burden of heart disease in the average general practice of some 2,500 persons in which there will be 275 middle-aged men. The family doctor can expect to be called to six clinical coronary cases each year at least, and one of these men will succumb. However, a survey of the other 'healthy' men will show these seven patients as only the tip of the iceberg. Below the surface a check-up would reveal many men (Table VIII) with small rises in blood pressure, in blood sugar and fat levels, many over-eating and over-smoking but not having to take the physical exercise of their forefathers either on the job or in getting to work. At least one in nine men will be addicted to consuming a packet of cigarettes each day. Each one of these personal characteristics doubles the risk of coronary disease in contrast to those men who have neither inherited nor acquired them.

VIII An average general practice
Coronary heart disease in 2765 middle-aged men 45–64

1 death each year
5 clinical cases

15 Diastolic B.P. 100+, or Systolic 180+
21 E.C.G. Left Ventricle+, and S.+T. changes
24 Borderline blood sugar tolerance
29 Serum Cholesterol 300 mg+

31 Cigarettes 20 per day+
40 Height under 5½ feet
55 Obese: wt 10%+
60 Skinfold Suprailiac 2 cm+
140 Moderate to severe Atheroma

200 Insufficient exercise or sedentary job

? Emotional stress

Family history of sudden death before age 60

With such increasing knowledge Professor J. N. Morris, writing in the *Lancet*, September 1966, feels 'there is a new optimism that the modern epidemic of ischemic heart disease of middle age can be controlled. . . . Public health campaigns relating to these causes – e.g. education on the dangers of cigarette smoking or on the need for sedentary workers to take regular exercise – could be effective. But the dominant hope today is that action at the stage of precursor pathology (hypertension and hypercholesterolaemia in particular) may still achieve true primary prevention. Individuals shown to be susceptible will be identified and prophylactic measures directed at them. Prevention will be translated into the clinical field. . . . In these terms, three-quarters of the total incidence is already a worthwhile prediction: this is the main community problem. Reduction of disease in this high-risk group to that of the remainder would reduce the overall incidence among the busmen by about half. And an individual risk over five years of one in seven (about five times that of the remainder) is already serious enough to warrant attempts at individual prevention . . . since the clinical disease is so common, it may be more practical to aim at combining mass campaigns with personal prophylactic treatment for those special individuals identified as early candidates for the disease.'

This is a real break in the dark clouds. Moreover, the screening of persons in high risk groups registered in a general practice for further surveillance, and encouraging healthier habits, if not active drug prophylaxis, may reduce the number of potential candidates or postpone for some years the first clinical attack. Such a strategy is due for testing in the field by existing groups in the community for monitoring other chronic handicapping or fatal conditions such as:

glaucoma – the rise in pressure inside the eyeball insidiously narrowing down the field of vision, with symptoms too late for a simple operation to restore full vision and leading to a main cause of blindness in late middle age.

diabetes – often first presenting with thrombosis in an artery in the leg, heart or brain or with retinitis or neuritis.

pyleonephritis – in women often masquerading as a simple recurring urinary infection but repeated damage to the kidney leads to its failure.

depressive mental illness – the commonest psychosis in middle and later life often leading to a successful suicide at the coroner's inquest – yet, like the other common examples, a chronic relapsing if often silent disease, the speed of whose downward course can be slowed down, if not stalled by modern tablets.

With such potential control available, why yet not applied? Perhaps medicine, as the second oldest profession and unchanged for centuries, finds it difficult to adapt its hoary institutions and traditional habits within two decades to such novel possibilities from the drug industry.

CANCER

As first killer, coronary heart disease is a new epidemic and still increasing (although in doctors it flattened out and may now be declining as they follow their own advice of less smoking and eating and more exercise). By contrast the second killer, cancer, has taken a remarkably steady toll of lives over the past four decades. Cancer of the breast has scarcely changed in its toll and is first cause of death in women, accounting for almost one-third of deaths in early middle age. Indeed, overall the cancer toll has been fairly static over the past decade as the falling rates from cancer of the stomach, gut and rectum are compensated by the increase in cancers of the lung, blood, pancreas and bladder of both sexes and in ovaries in women and prostate in men. However, the rise in deaths from lung cancer seems to have stopped in middle-aged men (and is declining for doctors of all ages). Its stationary peak is almost three times higher than Canada and twice as high as Scandinavia, so perhaps the saturation level of those at high risk has been reached in the middle aged whilst the older cohort continue to increase (Table IX).

The greatest reduction in the total cancer toll is, of course, immediately possible in cancer of the lung where a reduction in our natural addiction of cigarette smoking would reduce the bill by almost one half in men. But any natural addiction is difficult to switch, although sixth-formers and executives are already smoking less. Improved prospects for women are less feasible because cancer of the breast has no external

IX Cancer deaths in middle age in England and Wales 1965 (per million)

	Males		*Females*	
	45–54	55–64	45–54	55–64
LUNG				
Primary	624	2066	142	269
Unspecified	262	872	64	120
BREAST	1	8	577	824
Uterus cervix	—	—	191	200
other	—	—	57	139
Ovary and tubes	—	—	219	315
Prostate	22	162	—	—
Bladder	52	212	18	52
STOMACH	243	785	98	301
Colon	102	303	128	322
Rectum	79	251	57	160
Brain and C.N.S.	78	139	52	77
Blood lymphatic	143	273	90	185
Other cancer	434	1044	305	676
ALL CANCER	2040	6115	1998	3640

'cause' to be eliminated and is closely related to the biochemical soil on which its cells can flourish. However, studies in Guernsey women over the past five years suggest that the twenty per cent of the population having an abnormal excretion in their urine of steroid chemicals are two to three times more likely to develop breast cancer. Thus, as with the non-malignant diseases, a high-risk group at the precursor stage might be screened out for regular surveillance with the hope of adjusting the biochemical soil or of early X-ray detection for prompt treatment.

It is salutary to see from Table VII, in view of all the enthusiasm for Cervical Smearing, that women die more often from cancer of the lung, ovary and tubes, large bowel and stomach, than from the cervix. Nevertheless, regular health counselling and periodic checks are the most promising investment of the limited resources of any health service.

STROKES, BRONCHITIES AND VIOLENT DEATH

As with the overall cancer toll, there has been little change in the total deaths of these three corporals of death.

Despite the effective control of high blood-pressure by modern drugs, it is disappointing that death rates from strokes have changed so little over the past three decades. Again, the advent of antibiotics produced its miracles mainly in infancy and childhood and in pneumonia and other bacterial infections. In middle and later years with a lifetime of wear and tear on ageing tissues and with mixed virus infections, even the latest fashionable antibiotics are not a 'wonder cure'. Thus, the death toll in middle age from our own English disease of chronic bronchitis has shown little decline.

Despite a common impression, fatal accidents and violent deaths have not generally increased over the past 100 years, but, with the conquest of infections, they have risen in rank and life has become more valuable and less fatalistic. Of course, there has been a change in the type of accidents with the decline in those in mines and drowning being replaced by those on the road. However, it is remarkable that despite the increasing hazards in the speed and intricacy of modern machines and with road traffic increasing five-fold since 1930 and doubling in the past decade, that there has not been an overall increase in the fatal death toll. This reflects the advances in resuscitation, modern surgery, anaesthesia and control of infection. Indeed, if an accident victim today reaches hospital pulseless but with a heart flicker, he is likely to survive.

The first peak in fatalities in road accidents was in the mid thirties; after World War II hospital care reduced the toll but recently the death rate has climbed back to the same high pre-war level. It is, of course, the adolescent sons in their new freedoms of riding the tiger who kill themselves, whilst their middle-aged fathers turning fifty have the lowest rates for fatal traffic accidents of all male ages.

Trends in suicides are difficult to follow as it was still a crime and not a sickness until 1961. There was the usual fall in suicides during the war years, but after the war there was a rise at most ages until 1950 when a divergence appeared. In the last decade the female suicide rate has continued to rise at all ages, but the rate for men has only increased in those under forty-five, whilst in early middle age it is steady and in late middle age is falling. Despite this male decline at all ages, however, men take their own life more often than women.

HOSPITAL TREATMENT

Turning from the fatal risks to the hazards of admission to hospital, the lowest rates are in adolescence and young adulthood (except for childbirth in women), but the risk increases in middle age and onwards, so that one in fourteen women in the prime of life are admitted to hospital each year, and one in twelve men, and stay for about three weeks. The majority of these patients undergo general surgery and the success of operating in middle and later life is indicated, since three per cent of middle-aged people have a surgical operation each year.

The operations carried out are the common and unspectacular procedures. In men twelve per cent are repairing hernia, five per cent for varicose veins and four per cent each for haemorrhoids and simple skin excisions. Excluding the two per cent pneumoectomy, mainly for lung cancer, forty-two per cent are common procedures which by their very repair nature will have little direct influence on reducing death rates, although they will reduce disability and discomfort (Table X). In women, the load of repair is even more striking, with half of all surgery covered by only ten common procedures and indeed, twenty-eight per cent of all surgery is in the good hands of the gynaecologist (Table XI). Although peptic ulcer is declining as an epidemic (and for quite unknown reasons), it still is one of the main conditions

X Main surgical operations in middle-aged men: aged 45–64 (H.I.P.E. 1961) (per cent)

Inguinal hernia	12
Peptic ulcer	5
Varicose veins	5
Haemorrhoids	4
Skin excise	4
Gall-bladder	3
Prostate	3
Abdominal drain only	2
Appendix	2
Teeth	2
Lung	2
	44%

XI Main surgical operations in middle-aged women: aged 45–64 (H.I.P.E. 1961) (per cent)

Prolapse	11	
Total Hysterectomy	8	
D. & C. only	7	
Other Uterus	3	
		28%
Varicose Veins	6	
Gall-bladder	5	
Breast	4	
Appendix	4	
Skin	3	
Haemorrhoids	2	
Abdominal drain only	2	
		25%
		53%

for middle-aged men being admitted to hospital. Twice as many men as women in their prime enter hospital for treatment of haemorrhoids while the ratio is reversed for varicose veins.

The list of mainly medical conditions for middle-aged patients in hospital shows again the leading role of coronary heart disease in men and when strokes are added to it, the dominance of diseases of the arteries. Respiratory infections are a close second, but with the availability of weapons for the conquest of tuberculosis, it is not flattering that it still persists on a British hospital list of in-patients. The third group of conditions is the common ragbag of rheumatism and fibrositis as symptoms from the wear and tear on joints and spinal discs appearing in middle age.

Out of every hundred in-patients, 95 women and 92 men are discharged as only five per cent and eight per cent respectively die in hospital. This is some achievement considering the increasing severity of injuries, the twelve per cent of readmissions within a year often for increasingly critical relapses or recurrences, as well as all the new challenges being tackled by surgical teams today.

Clinical advances in the past decade in hospital are seen even more strikingly in the modern psychiatric hospital where active therapy replaces the old custodial care of the asylum. Thanks to new drugs, patients can be discharged within a few weeks even though half may have to be readmitted within twelve months. The shorter hospital stay preserves the social ties with the home. Middle age has fewer admissions to hospital than younger adults in their twenties and thirties, or in those after retiral. The risk of admission in middle age is highest for women in the 45–55 age group when it reaches 1 in 200 per year.

SICKNESS AT HOME AND AT WORK

To be admitted to hospital, most patients have to be referred by the family doctor and, indeed, it is he who takes care of over ninety per cent of the medical demands in the community.

On average, middle-aged folk have to see their G.P. once every two months. Indeed, the man in his prime is the most frequent attender of all males and he will be prescribed 36s. worth of drugs each year. (By contrast, retired men see the G.P. one-third less often than elderly ladies who are the most demanding of all.) This average conceals on the one hand the 20 per cent who do not see the doctor within the twelve months, but on the other hand there is the increasing number of familiar faces with chronic relapsing conditions which in middle age rises to almost twenty per cent of the G.P.s' list for men and thirty per cent for women (Table XII). The

XII Chronic* sick in general practice
(per cent of age-group on list)

Age	*Men*	*Women*
30–39	10	18
40–49	14	23
50–59	18	29
60–69	39	35
70–79	49	48
80+	71	62

*Patients with chronic or relapsing disorders or who were receiving treatment with drugs over at least a year.

actual complaints for which they attend is only too familiar – respiratory infections, influenza and chronic bronchitis, the aches and pains of fibrositis, and minor injuries account for the first one-third. The second third is a much longer list of some eighteen conditions. These include osteoarthritis, blood pressure, dyspepsia and other bellyaches which may well be only the 'visiting card' concealing underlying social tensions and difficulties in adjustment at work or within the home.

Indeed, these emotional problems may really account for one-third of the visits to the family doctor. Although some physical complaints are trivial and some not immediately serious, others, like emphysema and coronary heart disease and rheumatoid arthritis, do portend handicap at a later age. Indeed, already in late middle age the family doctor can see the beginnings of many pre-geriatric problems which only too often are delayed in their presentation and when rehabilitation is then so much more difficult.

The risks of chronic sickness in late middle age is also reflected in increasing sickness absence from work. In his forties, the average man is off work for two weeks but, in his mid-fifties, this doubles to four weeks and, rising sixty, to seven weeks (Table XIII). The outstanding medical reason for

XIII Sickness absence from work 1958

Age	Weeks sick	% population off over 3 months
40–	1·6	1·1
45–	2·1	1·6
50–	2·7	2·5
55–	4·1	3·3 to 6·9
60–	6·4	7·8 to 11·2

sickness absence is, of course, the English Disease, Chronic Bronchitis. After a decade or more of 'just a smoker's cough', the unskilled man in middle age finds his lungs are so damaged that he is short of breath when labouring. One winter, after his annual bout of Bronchitis, he is unable to go on as a navvy and without any skill to offer he has to look around for almost any light job as a sweeper-up or nightwatchman. Thus the bald graphs (Fig. 2) conceal the men incapacitated from work for over three months if not for the rest of their working life. This premature invalidity rises to seven per cent by age fifty-five and to ten per cent turning sixty. In this withdrawal from work into premature retirement, the man is deprived of his role as a wage earner and so suffers 'a little death' as he is forced to retreat from the company of his mates at work to feeling useless in the home and in the neighbourhood. It may be even worse when this is not due to sickness but to an

Fig. 2. Proportion of total deaths due to specified causes, by age group, males, 1962

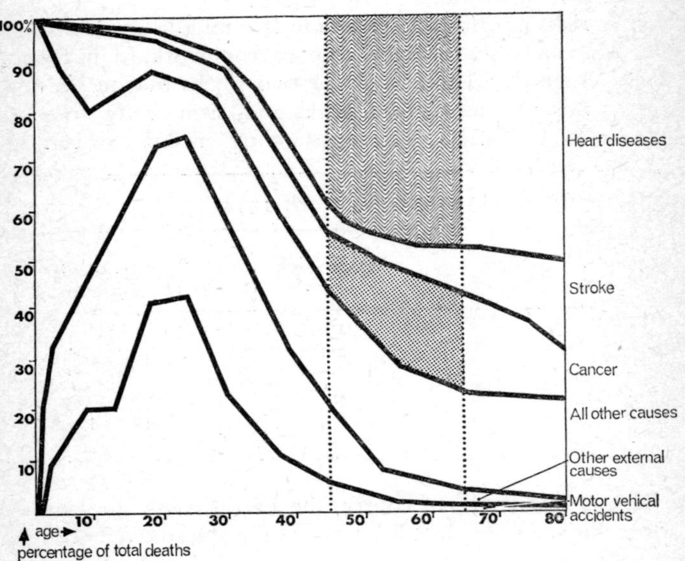

archaic inhuman rule at sixty-five. This compulsory retirement age is a hangover from the era of unemployment in the hungry 1930's, condoned by both Trade Unions and Industry today when manpower is scarce and when some other developed countries have raised the age to seventy. In late middle age society has already preordained much of the social isolation and loneliness which are at the core of the geriatric problems in the elderly. This deprivation of their working role for men in late middle age is their outstanding social hazard. When a man without a skill is unable to continue earning a wage in his late fifties and if his wife is also unable to work, the fall in the family income will soon eat into the provision of their basic needs of food and fuel. Social security supports are just not enough to fill many gaps in these years of inflation. If they live in the industrial north he will become more handicapped as he reaches his sixties. Should a spouse die then the downward spiral is given an extra twist. (Fig. 3)

Fig. 3. Proportion of total deaths due to specified causes, by age group, females, 1962

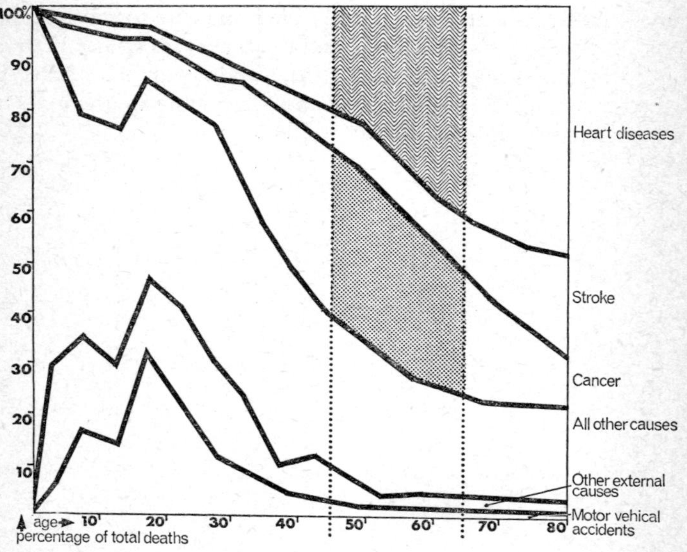

The core of the chronic handicapped and the mentally and socially sick is the toughest challenge to any health service (indeed few even undertake such responsibilities). In our system of values, prestige goes to the young and the prospering fit. A blind eye is turned against those without a job in days of full employment, against the poor and the handicapped when after middle age (but, interestingly such children involve our compassion). We meet these problems of the first impoverished leisure class in our history with mixed emotions. Our attitudes and actions are based more on our religious or humanitarian traditions rather than facing up to them with a critical social and medical analysis. It is probable that the very successes of modern medicine often mean survival, but on expensive maintenance therapy, for another more critical episode of clinical brinkmanship. Medicine and society will really have to think out how the limited resources of budget, of skill, and plant, can be put to give good care to most of the population, most of the time, and to all persons whose need is important. Society will look to the middle-aged as the generation of decision-makers – and they anyway themselves have a vested interest in the problem.

Health hazards 2
A glossary

A doctor

The following are brief descriptions of the diseases, how they come about, and the effects they cause. They are divided into diseases of men and women, but most of the disorders can occur in either sex, and the division is for the most part only an indication of which sex is more likely to be affected.

Diseases of men

CANCER is an abnormal growth of cells. They multiply free from controlling influences and quickly destroy the tissue from which they arise. The cancerous growth may arise in any organ in the body, and, by invading blood or lymphatic vessels can soon be spread to other parts of the body such as lung, liver, bones or brain. The organ of origin of the cancer is called the *primary* site, and the secondary spread of cells, to the liver for example, is called a *metastasis*. In men the common primary sites for cancer are the lung, stomach, prostate gland, and bowel.

LUNG CANCER This very common disease is largely preventable. It is unusual to find a patient with lung cancer who has not been a heavy smoker. The tumour may not present until it is well advanced, when coughing up blood, breathlessness or general ill health may take the patient to the doctor. Caught in time, a surgical cure may be possible. Too often the disease has metastasised to bone, brain, or liver, by the time medical advice is sought.

STOMACH CANCER The cause of this tumour, which arises in the lining of the stomach, is unknown, but genetic factors may play a part, while in some countries irritant foods are thought to be a causative factor. The tumour may be silent for many weeks, and then presents with loss of appetite and weight, or anaemia due to loss of blood into the stomach. Early surgery is sometimes curative, but spread to the liver and abdominal lymph glands occurs quickly.

PROSTATIC CANCER At the base of the bladder in men, is the prostate gland, surrounding the passage along which urine flows to the exterior. Enlargement of the prostate may cause difficulty in passing urine. Although the commonest cause of enlargement is not cancerous, malignant growths do occur. Spread to the spinal bones is common. Operation and hormone treatment have greatly improved the outlook for this disorder.

BOWEL CANCER After digestion in the small bowel, food residue travels to the large bowel, or colon, and thence to the rectum. Tumours of the bowel nearly always arise from the colon or rectum. While a few uncommon diseases predispose to these tumours, no cause is apparent in the majority of cases. The usual presentation is with diarrhoea or constipation, and the passage of blood or mucus. These tumours are usually amenable to surgery.

CORONARY ARTERY DISEASE The muscle of the heart is richly supplied with blood through the coronary arteries. If this flow of blood is blocked by disease, damage to the heart muscle will result. The commonest disease of these, and other, arteries is *atherosclerosis*. Sometimes referred to as 'hardening of the arteries', atherosclerosis is caused by the deposition of a fatty substance called atheroma in the arterlia wall. Obesity, diabetes, sedentary occupations, cigarette smoking and the rich diets of affluent societies, all predispose to atherosclerosis and coronary artery disease. When atherosclerosis occurs, the bore of the artery is narrowed and eventually there may be complete blockage of blood flow. The two main conditions which coronary atherosclerosis produces are *angina* and *coronary thrombosis*.

ANGINA This is the name given to a pain which arises from

the heart. It is due to an inadequate blood flow along the coronary arteries. The pain is often severe and is felt characteristically on exertion, when the heart is working hardest and its demand for the oxygen in the blood is greatest. Angina may continue for many years without any more serious effects.

CORONARY THROMBOSIS Strictly speaking this means a complete blockage of one of the coronary arteries. When this happens, heart muscle supplied by the artery, dies. Death of a tissue due to cutting off of blood supply is called infarction, so this condition is more correctly termed *myocardial* infarction. The severity of a myocardial infarction or 'coronary', depends on how much heart muscle dies. After one myocardial infarction there is the risk of a second if yet another artery gets blocked.

HIGH BLOOD PRESSURE The blood is pumped into the arteries with considerable force and the pressure this causes in the arteries is measured by the familiar blood pressure cuff. High blood pressure or *hypertension* simply means that this pressure is higher than normal for a particular age. The factors controlling blood pressure are very complex and there is no known cause in the majority of cases although it does tend to run in families. In a few cases hypertension results from kidney or hormonal disorders. Hypertension may be present for years without apparent ill effects, but the heart has to work harder against the increased pressure and starts to compensate by increasing in bulk. Later, if the blood pressure is not treated the heart enlarges further and begins to fail. At the same time the hypertension hastens the development of atherosclerosis, and coronary artery disease may add to the burden that the overworked heart has to bear. Hypertensive patients are prone to develop angina and coronary thrombosis.

PEPTIC ULCER Food passes into the stomach, and then, after digestion with strong acid, into the first part of the bowel called the duodenum. Peptic ulcer is the term used to describe ulcers in the stomach and duodenum. Duodenal ulcers occur in a younger age group than gastric (stomach) ulcers. The cause of the ulcers is not clear. Constitutional factors are of importance and so are emotional stresses. The peptic ulcer patient is often a tense, worrying, introspective person. An area of the lining of the stomach or duodenum becomes eroded and inflamed. The strong stomach acid, and the periodic contractions of the stomach during digestion, both cause pain if an ulcer is present. If the ulcer erodes deeply into the wall of the stomach or duodenum it may penetrate a blood vessel causing haemorrhage, or it may make a perforation in the wall allowing the gastric contents to spill out, causing peritonitis. Treatment of peptic ulceration is either medical or surgical depending on the stage the ulcer has reached.

RESPIRATORY DISEASES Inspired air passes through the windpipe into the bronchial tubes. These branch and divide until they end in minute inflatable air spaces. Atmospheric irritants are dealt with by the lungs through an elaborate defence mechanism. Cells lining the bronchi produce mucus in which irritant particles are trapped. The mucus is then coughed up out of the bronchi.

CHRONIC BRONCHITIS Cigarette smoking is probably the main cause of this crippling malady although atmospheric pollution plays a part. The constant inhalation of irritants together with chest infections inflame the bronchi, causing bronchitis. If the inflammation continues it passes into a chronic stage. The bronchi are damaged and the mucus-producing cells step up their activity and excess mucus is produced and expectorated. The smoker's cough is due to chronic bronchitis. The bronchi swell and their bore is narrowed and this obstructs the free flow of air, causing wheezing and breathlessness on exertion. Later as the damage continues, breathlessness is present at rest. Extra effort is needed to pump blood through the damaged lung, and after some years the heart begins to fail.

STROKES Any part of the brain will die if its blood supply

is interrupted. Depending on the part affected, the disturbance will cause paralysis, difficulty in speaking, convulsions, partial loss of vision or sensation, or impairment of intellect. These episodes are called strokes or cerebro-vascular accidents. They come about due to blockage of a cerebral artery by atheroma, or due to haemorrhage from a burst artery, or due to a clot of blood becoming lodged in an artery. High blood pressure and all the factors causing atherosclerosis predispose to strokes. The commonest form of stroke is that which causes paralysis and difficulty in speech. Recovery may be partial or complete, but there is the possibility of further strokes if other arteries are affected. With modern treatment the chances of recovery after a stroke have been greatly increased.

Diseases of women

ANAEMIA This means a deficiency of the amount of haemoglobin in the blood. There are a great many causes, but perhaps the commonest is blood loss. This is often due to excessive menstrual loss, or to bleeding from a peptic ulcer, or haemorrhoids. If there is no obvious cause, persistent anaemia may need to be carefully investigated before it can be put right. Hidden blood loss, vitamin deficiencies, infections and tumours may all present with anaemia. Since oxygen is carried by haemoglobin in the blood, anaemia may cause fatigue and breathlessness apart from obvious pallor of the skin.

ARTHRITIS simply means inflammation of a joint. In each joint, the bone ends are covered by well-lubricated cartilage. In long-standing arthritis, the cartilage may be destroyed, and deformity and painful grating of bone may occur. RHEUMATOID ARTHRITIS This disease may affect any joint in the body. Usually both sides of the body are affected symmetrically. It may involve only a few joints with minor disability, or it may be a very destructive disease involving almost every joint. The initial cause of the inflammation is unknown, but the arthritis appears to be self-perpetuating. There may be long periods of remission followed by a relapse. The disease may burn itself out, or it may go on for years with increasing disability, although modern treatment has meant that far fewer people are severely disabled than formerly.

OSTEOARTHRITIS This extremely common disorder is due to wear and tear on the joints and is therefore found in people who do heavy jobs, or who work a lot with their hands, or who have had a joint damaged by a previous injury. It is not really an inflammation, but is more a wearing out of cartilage, and for this reason it is often called degenerative joint disease. In most cases, this is only slowly progressive and as with rheumatoid arthritis, modern physiotherapy and orthopaedic surgery have transformed the outlook for these patients.

CANCER The breast, cervix and uterus are the main sites of malignant growth in women. The same general considerations apply as in tumours in men.

BREAST CANCER A lump in the breast, noticed by chance, may turn out to be cancer. If the tumour is attached to the skin it may pull on the nipple deforming it. Caught early the chances of surgical cure are very high. Later the tumour may spread to lymph glands and bone. Even then, radiotherapy and hormone treatment may give good results.

CERVICAL CANCER The neck of the womb or cervix protrudes into the vagina. Some cancers arising there have the extraordinary property of remaining in the primary site for years before spreading. If special scrapings are taken from the cervix, cancer cells can be seen under the microscope. At this stage a simple operation will be curative. This early detection of cancer of the cervix, is the object of 'screening' clinics where the scrapings are taken. At a more advanced stage surgery and radiotherapy may produce good results.

UTERINE CANCER The main part of the womb, or uterus, can also be the site of malignant tumours which commonly present as bleeding after the menopause, which may be mistaken for a period. A curettage, or scraping of the uterus will reveal the diagnosis and operation can be undertaken.

DIABETES Carbohydrate in the diet is digested and absorbed into the blood stream as glucose, where it is taken up by the cells as a source of energy. Insulin is a hormone which promotes sugar uptake by cells and also affects protein and fat metabolism. In diabetes there is a diminished activity of insulin, which in young diabetics is due to a deficiency of the hormone while in older diabetics it is usually due to a resistance to its action. Why some people develop diabetes is not known but genetic factors are very important. When there is insufficient activity of insulin sugar builds up in the blood and spills out in the urine. The deranged fat and sugar metabolism predisposes to atherosclerosis so that diabetics are more liable to develop coronary artery disease, strokes and poor circulation in the limbs, than most people. In addition damage to the kidneys and nerves may occur and there is an increased liability to develop cataracts. Many diabetics need to take insulin by injection but in middle-aged patients, who are often obese, diet alone may control this disorder.

GALL BLADDER DISEASE Bile manufactured in the liver is stored in the gall bladder. When food is emptied from the stomach the gall bladder contracts and expells bile along the bile duct.

GALL STONES are stones in the gall bladder. The reason for their formation is not known, but chronic inflammation and diabetes are predisposing causes. Many people have gall stones without symptoms, but irritation of the gall bladder may cause dyspepsia or a stone may lodge in the neck of the gall bladder or bile duct and then intense pain may occur. Obstruction to the flow of bile may cause jaundice. Removal of the stones and gall bladder will cure these symptoms.

OPHTHALMIC DISEASE The globe of the eye is like a camera. Light passes through the cornea, and is focused by the lens. The image falls on the sensitive retina and is transmitted to the brain. The globe is filled with fluid under pressure which keeps it tense. Both men and women are affected by diseases of the eye.

CATARACTS are opacities of the lens. They usually occur in old age but diabetics may develop them earlier on. When they interfere with vision, the opaque lens can be removed.

DETACHED RETINA The retina may come adrift from the back of the eyeball and when this happens vision is impaired. The detachment often occurs without obvious cause, but very severe short-sightedness predisposes to this disease. In recent years many methods have been devised for fastening the retina back down to the globe helping to prevent further detachment.

GLAUCOMA This means a rise in pressure in the eyeball as a result of blockage of the outflow of the fluid within it. The onset may be sudden with intense pain, or gradual, with slow loss of vision. Inflammatory diseases in the eye, predispose towards this condition, which is improved by operations which restore the drainage of fluid.

PSYCHIATRIC DISEASES At any age people may suffer from anxieties and tensions which are not severe and which do not take them to the doctor. When more pronounced these feelings may profoundly interfere with the enjoyment of life. Two major psychiatric disorders in middle age, are depression and dementia.

DEPRESSION Everyone feels depressed on occasions, and after personal tragedy, grief and depression are normal. Depression is considered to be abnormal, when there is no apparent cause or when the depth of depression is out of all proportion to the precipitating event. Some women, during and after the menopause, become depressed for no apparent reason. This is sometimes called Involutional Melancholia. Feelings of guilt and unworthiness occur, and suicide may be attempted. Modern treatment has greatly improved the outlook of this disorder.

DEMENTIA This means impairment of intellect, and is a symptom of many diseases. If often accompanies advanced age, but may appear prematurely as a result of disease of cerebral arteries especially atherosclerosis. Failure of memory and concentration occur and episodes of confusion are common. With modern drugs and care, the patient may remain independent for many years.

PART 3 MENTAL POWERS

Middle age: what happens to ability?

R. M. Belbin

Dr R. M. Belbin graduated in Psychology at Cambridge in 1948 and then became a Research Worker in the Unit for Research into Problems of Ageing at Cambridge. He was awarded his Ph.D. in 1952 for his thesis 'The Employment of Older Workers in Industry'. For the past ten years he has worked as an independent management consultant. He is currently engaged in carrying out demonstration projects for O.E.C.D. in the training of older workers in Sweden, Austria, U.S.A. and United Kingdom.

The natural fear of adults as they age is of a loss in their physical and mental powers. Many may wonder what truth there can be behind the saying 'too old at 40'. Some feel most confident that their abilities are as good as ever and feel indignant that prejudice exists against middle-aged people in some forms of employment. For others, middle age is the period at which they are at the height of their achievement and enjoy all the fruits of their mature abilities, personal satisfaction, good income and respect from work-mates and colleagues.

The great differences that exist between people might suggest that there was no underlying pattern in the way in which abilities change in middle age. This would be a mistaken conclusion because, although people's initial aptitudes, characteristics and experience differ, there are basic similarities in the sort of changes that are occurring, just as there are basic similarities in the change from babyhood to childhood in spite of the big individual differences between children.

The important thing for a person approaching middle age is to take a realistic view of the prospects. Many of the changes are irreversible and therefore the need is to adapt to them successfully. The significance of the changes that occur varies for each person according to the way he lives.

How significant are the losses in man's senses?

Man's capacity in middle age must be limited in some fields by the changes affecting the senses. In general there is a loss of sensitivity and/or a restriction in the range over which sensitivity is retained.

Take the efficiency of vision which may be measured in terms such as visual acuity (the amount of fine detail that can be perceived), convergence, accommodation and so forth. Ageing invariably brings about in the forties some loss in comparison with the twenties, in whatever manner visual efficiency is measured, usually of the order of ten per cent. Sometimes the loss is greater. The decrease in size of pupil, for example, means that between twenty and forty something like a third more brightness is required to compensate for the loss of light reaching the retina of the eye.

Hearing also provides evidence of loss. The capacity to respond to the upper frequency limits of sound (which is not usually demanded in everyday life) is curtailed by some ten per cent between twenty and forty. Other senses, about which reliable data exist, also show losses by the age of forty, although these losses are sometimes only small.

Man is undoubtedly past his peak by forty as an organism for receiving through his senses information about his environment. Thousands of years ago, and to a lesser extent even a century ago, this must have been a serious limitation in his everyday activities. The impact nowadays is relatively slight. A person engaged in competitive sport might feel that he had lost his 'eye', but others are not seriously affected. A deficiency in vision may readily be overcome by spectacles, a loss of sensitivity by improving the level of illumination at the work place. Man's control over his environment usually allows him to work comfortably within the capacity of his senses, even though important changes are taking place in middle age.

The danger lies in a failure to recognize that these limitations exist and that something needs to be done. Someone who finds reading a slight strain may prefer to shun reading matter with consequent long-term effects on the extent to which he maintains his educational status and keeps abreast of developments in his occupational area. The repercussions of changes in the senses are often of more importance than the absolute losses involved.

Physical strength and ability

Most people by middle age may be more conscious of a loss in physical energy than in the capacity of their senses which may even have passed unnoticed. It is all too apparent, for example, that middle-aged men are less keen to play football (though they may be enthusiastic about watching it).

The scientific evidence does confirm a loss in physical strength. Thirteen published studies concerned with the strength of various muscle groups over a wide age span all show a peak in strength in the twenties. By the forties the decline is mostly of the order of five–seven per cent, when the measure is the maximum strength which a given set of muscles can exert.

As with the senses, the fall in muscle strength seems of only marginal significance in everyday life. Few situations present themselves in which maximum exertion is required. The car, the labour saving devices in the household, mechanical handling in the factory and many other instances of the replacement of manpower by horsepower have transformed the demands of work, the normal drudgery of existence and with them the physical effects of becoming middle-aged.

The struggle to keep on top of the job

Often it is not man's physical grip that seems to matter; rather it is man's grip on his job. This is where skill, intelligence and general employability count. Here the evidence is more encouraging. Industrial studies have shown that once skills are satisfactorily learned there is little sign of loss in the forties and fifties, while employees usually show improvements in conscientiousness, time-keeping and absence of spoiled work. But what happens when man is confronted with the need to acquire new skills and respond to the demands of new work situations?

There are a good many problems that arise in this area. Yet there is one basic problem that is often left out of account: this relates to the capacity of the mind to organize the information received from the senses, especially information of a type that the mind does not normally receive and which cannot therefore be assisted by 'pre-coding'. Difficulties here are often mistakenly attributed to the deficiencies of the senses themselves.

The following illustration of the way in which losses in performance transcend losses in the senses comes from an experimental study of subjects engaged on an inspection task. The ages of the subjects ranged from twenty to forty-five but they were all matched for eyesight on a number of tests. They were then given sheets of paper on which were printed a number of broken rings and were instructed to cancel with a pencil each ring that had a break in a certain direction. In spite of the fact that subjects in their forties were not inferior in their vision they were not able to cancel so many rings correctly as the younger subjects in the given time. When the rings were very small, the illumination low and the contrast characteristics of rings and paper poor the differences with age became more marked. Even under the most favourable conditions the middle age group did not equal the performance of the younger. The central processes of the brain mechanism are in some way involved.

Situations which demand quickness in physical responses produce problems that have similar features. The explanations that are commonly given for the difficulties that are experienced are all too frequently attributed to the muscles and limbs rather than to the brain and the central nervous systems. It is instructive to examine a typical case in factory work. A well-established fact is that it is very difficult to train women on high speed sewing machine operations to reach the required standards except within the early years of adulthood. Most firms have found it necessary to impose some form of age barrier, usually thirty and quite often twenty-five, although exceptions are readily made for those with any relevant previous experience. The problems encountered can hardly be explained by citing the fact that people slow up as they get older. There is plenty of information available to show that the slowing up of speed of reactions is only small by the forties, hardly sufficient to affect materially the operations in question. In any case this type of slowing up is not shown by experienced women and machinists who stay on into their forties and fifties and generally perform in speed and quality as well as women in their twenties. The crux of the problem seems to be one of central brain function of learning to coordinate a pattern of signals with a pattern of responses. By developing training methods designed to reduce the severity of the 'information overload' that arises in this type of situation it has been possible to reduce a good deal of the limitations associated with age.

Other jobs require different types of ability. Just as age has a bearing on the capacity to acquire certain types of manual skill in industry so it has a relevance also to 'mental' skills. This may be seen by looking at some high-level forms of work in relation to age.

Inventiveness and intelligence

Some interesting facts have been presented by H. C. Lehman[1] who once made an exhaustive study of the productivity of distinguished persons in a wide variety of intellectual, cultural and scientific pursuits. Lehman listed the outstanding work

[1] H. C. Lehman. *Age and Achievement*, Princeton University and O.U.P. 1953.

of persons operating in fields ranging from Chemistry and Mathematics to Opera and Ballad writing. He found that the peak period of output came in the thirties in fourteen of the sixteen different fields studied. The forties became the second most productive age, but the fifties, were less than half as productive as the thirties.

Taking the criterion of people's best work Lehman found that the peak period came earlier than the most productive period usually by half a decade, but sometimes by rather more. For example, in literature the most productive period is in the age group 40–44 but the peak period for an author's most outstanding work is much earlier at 25–29. Lehman also made analysis of output in relation to age for science and mathematics with the object of comparing the differences in cultural background. He compared Russians, Englishmen, Italians, Frenchmen, Germans and Americans but found the age trends very similar. The maximum was achieved between thirty and forty with a fairly steady drop for each decade thereafter, although many still managed to produce original work in the seventies and eighties. Some individuals like Edison, went on inventing in bursts of creation, throughout their life span.

A sizeable proportion of the population lies between the two groups that have been discussed, that is between manual workers and persons of outstanding distinction. For this middle group it might be useful to consider the subject of intelligence, since this is of importance over a wide range of occupational abilities.

'Intelligence' is usually measured by one of the many forms of intelligence test. However, it has been established that familiarity with intelligence tests can have the effect of improving scores. As middle-aged people are less conversant with them than younger adults so it would follow that the true scores of middle-aged adults may be under-represented. Leaving this qualification aside we must note that 'intelligence' does show a downward trend by the forties on average in most of the studies that have been reported.

Average figures taken alone, however, are capable of being misleading. They do not necessarily imply that the trends are the same for all individuals. Fuller investigation of the results reported show that the differences within an age group increase as age advances, so that while some are achieving scores comparable with the more able of the younger groups, others gain very poor scores.

There is also evidence from experiments where people have been retested over a time span to show that those who were the more intelligent on the initial test maintain their intelligence well, while the less intelligent show the greater signs of decline. In 1950, one American researcher retested 127 college graduates who had originally been tested in 1919. The test material could be classified in eight basic types. On four of these the scores were approximately equivalent to those gained thirty-one years earlier, but on the other four significant improvements in score were recorded. It would seem from this that college educated people are inclined to maintain their intelligence well.

Some of the loss in intelligence that is registered on *average* scores in middle age may be linked with ill health. This might be deduced from the studies that have been made on retired persons which have shown that there the differences in 'intelligence' amongst apparently fit people are linked with the presence and absence of sub-clinical symptoms. Those who have minor symptoms are less 'intelligent' than those in very good health. Since health tends to decline with age it is to be expected on this ground alone that small losses in mental power may tend to become evident in middle age. But this would not follow for those who retain good health.

The importance of continued learning

Another factor which seems of importance in the preservation of mental ability is the extent to which this ability is exercised in practice.

One study of a group of mature adults attending a teachers'

training course showed that those who had been members of other courses since their formal education ceased achieved better examination results than those who had not. Another comparable result was shown in a recent nationwide study of persons undergoing a course of training for a Boiler Operator's Certificate. The examination consisted of both practical and theoretical sections. A personal questionnaire was filled in by the trainees and from this it emerged that while many had engaged in no form of educational activity since leaving school, some had taken an interest in other activities involving learning, attending courses on musical appreciation, trade union affairs and so on. On the practical examination there was no difference between the two groups, indicating that the groups in general ability and experience were comparable, but on the theoretical section of the examination the 'experienced learners' achieved appreciably better results than the others, although the type of learning upon which they had been engaged had no obvious relevance to the examination.

It has already been stated that acquired skills are normally well maintained in middle age and beyond. But mature people cannot live entirely on their reserves, i.e. the abilities and special skills acquired in youth, without eventually encountering the type of crisis in which their specific abilities gained long ago are no longer required and are not appreciated. If, however, people have continued to acquire knowledge and engage in various forms of learning and training, there will be elements in their experience that are likely to help them to adapt to new situations. In this way the accumulation of what has been learned can more than compensate for loss of learning ability.

Many people, however, by middle age have allowed themselves to sink into a restricted environment in which their activities are largely matters of routine. Situations that demand new learning and new experience are largely avoided. Such conditions are likely to have unfavourable influence on mental faculties.

As a general statement it would seem that how adults spend

their middle years has a major bearing on the characteristics of ageing especially in their psychological and social forms.

Marginal losses and continued opportunity

In conclusion, it might be useful to place the facts presented into some form of perspective. The process of ageing will be seen by the forties to have already imposed certain constraints on performance and to have affected certain faculties. For most people these limitations have only a marginal influence on their lives.

The physical characteristics of ageing have no more than a tenuous connection with 'Ability' in the general sense which is largely a matter of the special skills that people have learned and developed. In fact, by middle age the non-physical aspects of ageing loom up, perhaps, as the more important. The extent to which adults are able to maintain their flexibility of mind, to adjust themselves to a changing world and to the new demands in the work situation have more bearing on the problems of everyday life than losses in the sensitivity of the sense organs or muscle power. It is known that physical exercise has a favourable influence in offsetting some of the physical symptoms of ageing. What is now becoming increasingly apparent is that mental exercise has an equal part to play in resisting those unfavourable aspects of ageing which colour the very term 'middle age'.

A current problem of the middle-aged: retraining in industry

Eunice Belbin

Dr E. Belbin graduated in Cambridge in 1948. She then joined the research staff at the Experimental Psychology Laboratory, Cambridge, working under Sir Frederic Bartlett. She gained a Ph.D. in 1953 and since then has conducted research for the Medical Research Council and the Department of Scientific and Industrial Research. She is currently the Director of the Research Unit into Problems of Industrial Retraining, University College, London, and is a member of the Government's Central Training Council and of its Research Committee.

She and Dr R. M. Belbin have two children and live in Cambridge.

Learning a new industrial skill is a challenging task at any time. For the middle-aged worker, however, whose own skill has become redundant and who is separated by some twenty-five years from his previous learning experience, the problems can become quite acute. Yet if Britain is to make efficient use of its manpower, there is little doubt that the shortages of skilled labour hampering certain growth industries will have to be met from the reserve of older workers made available by the rapid march of technological change.

No one likes to think of a treasured possession becoming obsolete, least of all the skilled worker who not only finds his livelihood disappearing but also his self-esteem. Moreover, he sees himself as seriously handicapped in competing for jobs with his younger colleagues. He has less formal education than those who completed their schooling more recently and his educational background is less likely to be keyed to current occupational demands.

Too old at thirty-five

Perhaps one of the most serious handicaps to his re-employment in skilled work is the current attitude of many industries to taking on for training anyone over the age of thirty-five. For example, it is said that in the Computer industry 11,000 systems analysts are required in the next three years. Industrial advertisements for analysts, however, emphasize the importance of Youth; '. . . if you are between the ages of twenty-three and thirty-three, here's your chance . . .' In fact, many of the new job opportunities which are being brought about by modern technology are particularly restrictive against the middle-aged entrant. The question is how justified are these attitudes?

One of the hobbies and rewards of a research worker in psychology is to explode widely held myths about members of the human species. As a result of studies both in the laboratory and in industry on the abilities, the difficulties and the potential of middle-aged men and women learning new skills, it is now possible to say '*not* too old at 40'!

But it is also true to say that where little or no acknowledgement has been made of the changing attitudes and abilities of the middle-aged, then there will be many falling by the wayside at a '40-plus' examination. This has become evident both from observing the process of retraining in a number of industries and from comparing the effectiveness of different experimental methods on groups of middle-aged workers.

Fear of failure

One of the major problems in training the middle-aged is to overcome initial anxiety. Educationalists would be in common agreement that learning is more effective when the learner is calm and confident. What is less well-known is that older people are more prone to anxiety in a learning situation than are their younger colleagues. Research has shown, for example, that if blood tests are taken before, during and after learning sessions, then the level of the free fatty acid content in the blood plasma (a sensitive measure of stress) differs according to age. Older people not only show greater stress during learning, but they remain under stress for a longer period afterwards. It has also been shown that a rise in free fatty acid level can be related to poor learning performance.

It is not difficult to see the relevance of this research result to industrial retraining. A good example could be cited from the engineering firm, Guest, Keen and Nettleford, who decided to train some of their redundant labour as toolsetters. This was an ambitious project: not only were the men in question labourers with little technical experience or expertise, they were also all over the age of fifty. It seemed initially that the men's apprehension and anxiety might completely mar the project. It needed a sympathetic understanding of their problems to get them started at all. The first few days, for example, were spent away from the machines, getting them used to the atmosphere and giving them very simple tasks in order to inculcate a feeling of success. Eventually, the project was hailed as an all-round success '. . . these men have gained great satisfaction from achieving a higher trade status . . .' instead of, as one trainee put it, 'being thrown on the scrap heap at fifty.'

Another organization found that an older recruit to training was unable to assimilate any of the information given to him. He found himself older than and of inferior education to all other members of the group. He sat glumly and without response until a point in the course when slide rules were introduced. 'I can use a slide rule' he said with some pride. From that point of gaining confidence he progressed and received a good average end-of-course mark.

Older trainees have a multiplicity of background experiences – and as many different starting points for learning any skill. If some of their experience can be recognized, appreciated and built upon their confidence will increase and their anxiety be allayed.

A number of other examples could be quoted from industry where failure of the older trainee to learn in the early stages was accurately diagnosed as a symptom of anxiety. Sometimes this can be minimized by keeping together a social or working group – a practical possibility if a firm is retraining its own personnel, but not so easy when, say, a firm in a development area is taking on green labour for training.

'New-boy' anxiety is the first of many difficulties experienced by the older recruit. While some organizations take pains to understand and to overcome the problems of their older retrainees, the majority of firms both here and abroad train their older recruits with substantially the same techniques as are used with younger trainees. In the light of differing ability with age, it is not surprising to find a heavy drop-out from the higher age groups. What is encouraging, however, is to find that, provided the training programme *is* adapted to the requirements of the older learner, then he often learns as well as – and sometimes better than – a younger recruit. What *are* his requirements?

Longer training sessions

Middle-aged trainees often show reluctance to leave a training session or to have a break to prevent fatigue. Surprisingly, they tend to continue beyond the point at which the younger recruits give up. This may be because they set higher standards and like to feel a sense of accomplishment or completion. It is also because a mature adult's short-term memory suffers relatively more from the distractions of other activities. It is therefore beneficial that he should continue at a task until the learning is thoroughly consolidated.

This is not to say that he needs overall a longer learning time. For example, an experiment was conducted with trainee teachers. They were given (with the use of a teaching machine) a five-hour course on map reading. Seventy-two prospective teachers helped with the experiment – some were recruits straight from school at a Teachers' Training College, others were 'mature students' training to be teachers. It was found that the young trainees performed their best with ten half-hour sessions. The older trainees under these conditions were significantly worse than the youngsters. Nevertheless, when five one-hour sessions were provided for the 'over thirty-fives' their final test performance was comparable with that of the younger trainees. Thus, the older trainees learned as much as the younger ones only when they had fewer but longer sessions.

Avoiding errors

On the whole, the middle-aged person is excessively cautious during learning, being reluctant to venture a response in times of doubt – perhaps for fear of recognizing his inadequacy. This means that he has to be pretty sure of himself when he does respond. Accordingly, it is often very difficult to get him to 'unlearn' any errors. It is particularly important, therefore, to ensure that he doesn't make any! The work must be planned carefully to ensure good comprehension and in stages of increasing difficulty.

But it must also set a challenge; an older learner dislikes material designed for children as much as an illiterate teenager would abhor learning to read from books written for five year olds.

'Unlearning' presents problems, too, in acquiring new skills which are modifications of an old skill. Experiments have shown that whereas younger people may benefit from previous experience, it often impedes the learning progress of the over forties. In certain circumstances, therefore, it may be better for a middle-aged man or woman to learn an entirely new skill.

Freedom from time stress

Time stress or 'pacing' has a far greater effect on performance as we age. This is thought to account for the large number of people who move off conveyor line work in their middle working years. While an older person may be well able to complete or to learn a task in a given time – or several tasks in succession – his performance often becomes disrupted when this 'given time' is imposed continuously by mechanization or by other people in a working group. One solution in a training school is to stagger the entry of the older learners and to minimize formal testing. In this way, the older learner is not forced to race against others or against time limits. One well-established training school has a policy of giving 'x' weeks of training, irrespective of age. If at the end of the **x** weeks the trainee fails the final test, he is allowed an extension of time. It is not surprising to find that many older people fail, and that many refuse the extension. The 'paced' situation within rigid time limits inhibits their progress; the examination takes its toll of the over-anxious; and once having failed, there is little confidence left to continue. On the other hand, in some research conducted on the training of sewing machinists it has recently been shown that, in training situations devoid of stress, older learners make the grade with surprising ease.

Adequate motivation

The older person needs greater stimulation than the young if he is to respond as well. If a light is shown to young and older people, the older person will appear to have seen a less intense light. This is true for most stimulation of the senses; it appears also to be true of learning behaviour. The middle-aged learner needs greater 'arousal'. The fact that he is likely to have greater personal responsibilities and distractions, means that he requires a much more stimulating programme of training if it is to excite his interest and hold his attention. Some of the newer teaching aids and techniques have proved useful in this respect.

Discovery learning

Both teaching machines and job simulators, which are receiving acclaim in many industrial retraining departments are important in creating 'arousal' in adults. The *method* of teaching, however, is perhaps even more important in this respect than the 'hardware'. Several experiments have now been conducted to show that Discovery Learning has special benefits for the middle-aged.

In a recent experiment to teach the principles of electricity to steam train drivers two methods of training were compared. The first, the traditional blackboard and lecture technique, took longer and was less effective for older trainess than a new experimental method.

The new method involved discovering the functions of different electrical components in a circuit by being presented with a series of problems to which it was necessary to supply answers. The over forties trained by this method showed marked superiority over the other older groups both in learning the course material and in transferring their knowledge to a broader area involving diagnosis of electrical faults. Furthermore, this older group trained by a Discovery Method were as good as (and, on two out of three final tests, better than) a group of young trainees taught by the classroom method.

This result has been reproduced in a number of industrial situations – invisible mending of worsted cloth, inspection of printing faults, retraining of builders to become stonemasons, and in a series of engineering jobs, including operation of a lathe. In all cases the Discovery Method has proved superior to a traditional method and has raised the standard of the over forties performance to that of younger groups. Discovery Learning is a technique more familiar to enlightened educational projects than it is to industry. Yet paradoxically it seems more appropriate to industry than to the School or University because its relative advantage increases with age.

The future

Many of the social and psychological problems associated

with teaching the middle-aged seem, then, to have some solution. Many of them are not a function of age as such but rather of experience – or lack of experience. Many industrial workers in their forties and fifties lacked opportunities in early education and have since become mentally inflexible due to lack of practice in learning; many, because of their lack of practice and fear of the unknown are more anxious than they need be. But in the changing society of today with its technological demands creating a need for a flexible and skilled labour force, training will *have* to be a continuous process. Everyone should have ample opportunity both for acquiring and maintaining the skill of learning. It is to be hoped that training and retraining will be so much the done thing that the individual will cease to fear it and cease to regard it as a symptom of his own shortcomings. At this point in time we should cease to write about the 'Problems' of the middle-aged learner.

PART 4 ROLES

The middle-aged wage-worker

F. Le Gros Clark

F. Le Gros Clarke was educated at Balliol College, Oxford before the First World War. Since then he concentrated on sociological research, and carried out studies on malnutrition, unemployment, population growth and agriculture. After the last war he carried out a world survey for the U.N. on school feeding provisions. Recently he has specialized on conditions on the factory floor and in the Trade Unions. His latest publications include *Work, Age and Leisure*, and *Growing Old in a Mechanized World*.

A *middle-aged* worker . . . the image conveyed has often little bearing on a man's status as an operative or a craftsman. Most workers would hesitate how to define such a man except in rather vague terms. The truth is that, where men are organized in groups for productive processes, what counts with them is the almost imperceptible change in personal relations that goes on with time between one individual and another; and of course age does play some part in it. Probably this has always been the case with human beings whenever they cooperated in running the economic affairs of a tribe or a primitive village. When young fellows or newcomers are drafted into the working of a factory, they find themselves faced with a medley of conventional attitudes, customs, codes of behaviour and mutual obligations, that have to be gradually assimilated; and these are embodied not only in the functions of charge hands and foremen, but more subtly in the ways of thought that were established by the men who have been long on the job. It is like a 'club'. For some time the new entrant does not express himself in the interchanges that take place on the shop floor or in a Trade Union branch; or if he ventures to do so, he may be neatly ignored. At last the period comes when he is fully accepted into the 'club'.

But at the farther end of the age scale the day will usually come when a man overhears himself referred to as 'old so-and-so'; and he knows then that he has ceased industrially to be middle-aged. A certain mild tolerance begins to be shown him by his supervisors and his fellow workers. He notices that at Union meetings the floor is now dominated by men in the prime of life with growing families. Many of his acquired skills or dexterities may have become partly outmoded. As gracefully as he can, he falls more and more silent in shop floor discussions.

There is no precise age span separating these two extremes. It is the age span of the industrial 'club', and that includes a very large number of men who would admit to being middle-aged. Because of their experience they claim a considerable share in perpetuating the customs and mutual obligations that help to govern factory affairs. It is they who especially personify the spirit of the working group – the spirit that determines the modes of work that a body of manual employees holds to be fair and proper. They will try to initiate the younger men into their codes, however acclimatized these latter are to new methods and more sophisticated machinery.

Contemplate for a moment the scene on the shop floor, in the colliery or on the building site. The smooth organization of the work is the job of foremen and departmental supervisors. If the statistics are reliable, there must be near half a million of these in England and Wales; and preponderantly they are middle-aged men. That is to say, at least three-quarters of them range in age from close to forty to a little above sixty. Incidentally, the proportion of mature forewomen is even larger; somewhere around four-fifths of them are of similar ages. As for such foremen and forewomen, it must be remembered that in many instances they will have been long familiar with their coevals among the employees. There has grown up between them a guarded intimacy, a relationship that fades in and out of temporary hostility. It is a kind of game, the rules of which are usually well enough understood by both sides. Again, a middle-aged worker often has qualities of his own for some of the operations of a factory or on a building site. A good many building foremen seem to agree that men of that generation can be trusted to set a steady persistent rhythm of work. A shop foreman, responsible as he is for deploying his labour effectively, will rarely admit that men in their fifties are not earning a reasonable wage.

There was one recent inquiry carried out near London, where a number of foremen in neighbouring factories were asked to make individual assessments of the capacity of more than 500 men in their fifties and beyond. Whatever the ages of the men, the foremen did not rank more than eight per cent of them as comparatively 'poor' workers. A good many of the older men had been or were in process of being moved to less arduous jobs, though this seemed unlikely to happen to a man much before sixty; but in any case, since foremen had mostly helped to initiate the transfer, they felt bound to claim that the change had been a successful one. That at all events was the impression left upon the investigator; and as a matter of fact, the very detailed inquiries made revealed few signs of a deterioration in performance until men were approaching their pensionable age.

Yet have we not here a glimpse of industrial conditions that may already be passing? For I suspect that the style and the average age of the foremen themselves is undergoing a gradual change. Much the same could apply to the average age at which exuberant and impatient younger men are accepted as full members of the working group of a department or a Union branch. As I have suggested, you can never affix a precise age to this admission into the inner 'club'. The age groups tend to shift as techniques are modified or revolutionized in one industry or another. Time was no doubt when the balance of ages in production was much more traditional; but to see what that was like we should have to study the survivals among us of small one-man establishments. As it happens, there are still a million or more of men spread over the country, who either work on their own account or as worker-masters employ a few men under them. We know from

Census returns a good deal about them; and it seems clear that more than five-sixths of these self-employed men are beyond the age of thirty-five or forty. The usual assumption is that up to that age they had been apprentices or working members of the family – or else that about that time of life they quit normal industry and take their chance as self-employed men. Far fewer women are in the same situation, the majority of them as small shopkeepers, hairdressers, dressmakers and so on; but an even larger proportion of them are over forty years. We cannot be sure whether in reality it is because these men and women represent an ageing and so a dying part of our economy. We only know that their numbers have remained fairly constant over the last twenty or thirty years. The point is that *pre-industrial* Britain probably presented a very similar age structure in the production and the distribution of goods.

But of course working communities have always had to face up to the conundrum of age; and until births were registered, it was never possible to measure a man's age transitions in years. Peoples devised ingenious ways for marking the passage into maturity and later on into middle life. We still have the residue of such ancient practices in various of the tribal communities of East Africa. They are mostly herdsmen by habit, or at any rate were so in the recent past; and it must be noted that beside the job of herding cattle they would have indulged occasionally in raiding or fighting expeditions. Also for the most part they believed in encouraging rather close fraternities among men of about the same age; with the result that everyone in the same 'age group' would move on together into the next grade, though there might in reality be differences of ten or more years among them. The work they might be called upon to perform fixes the role of the young adults of a tribe. They are the warriors; and they would remain at that grade until at ages ranging, we may suppose, from thirty-five to fifty a whole group of them are promoted to 'elders'. That is the term by which European anthropologists ordinarily denote the grade; but they are more like what we should call the 'middle-aged'. The truly *old* members of a tribe are another matter; and in some cases they retire to a little adjoining hamlet of their own. But the elders remain the repositories of the traditions and customs of a community.

An example of this kind is more remote in space than in essence from the factory floor. The advantage under such simple and primitive conditions was that the tough and dangerous tasks committed to the young men of a tribe distinguish them in a rough-and-ready way from those who had been relegated to the next honoured age grade. Moreover, the social and the economic aspects of a tribal community are indissolubly mixed up together, whereas in an advanced industrialism the two streams of life tend to flow in distinct channels. In Western Europe a man or woman might socially acknowledge middle age when, say, their children are well grown, their own parents dead or becoming progressively frail; yet on the job or in a Trade Union their activities may be basically much the same as they were twenty years ago. Nevertheless they have been long accepted into the broad age group of responsibilities, that stretches through middle life or even a little beyond. What, then, are the characteristics of this extended group for a wage-worker? First, it has *group* ways of thinking about his rights and obligations, in the sense that it is not merely composed of individuals each with his private and domestic incentives. Today its members feel in an organized if incoherent manner in terms of shop stewards, Trade Union representatives, industrial negotiations and joint industrial councils. Their minds combine two features of the work process. On the one side, they usually have a keen appreciation of efficiency on the job. A man ought, they hold, to be a good operative or craftsman or labourer – not a slacker, not ham-fisted, not the kind of fellow who is always complaining of his tools or working conditions. On the other side, there is such a thing as 'a fair day's work for a fair day's pay'; and this idea extends, we may say, to the week's and the year's work. A man who sets what is conceived as too high a working pace simply for his own private ends is frowned upon; so is a man prepared to work for unduly long hours or to take a wage lower than the accepted norm; so for the matter of that is a young man who grows irritated with the relatively circumspect movements of an older mate. Led by its middle-aged members, a gang or group of workers can be very tolerant of the 'slowing down' process observable in its older men. It may rather unwillingly restrain its overall *tempo* of work on their behalf; and it will certainly assign to them the less arduous duties if that be possible.

Such are the modes of thought commonly met with on the shop floor, on the docks or on a building site; and they are quite distinct from the image of a manual worker still held by some economists and some employers. These tend to think of him and his mates as a body of individualists, each only trying to maximize his personal earnings. The modes of thought of which I speak are relatively modern. They reflect among other things the worker's urgent desire to have a guaranteed tenure of employment, to avoid redundancies or at the worst to bargain for compensatory payments. They reflect, too, the aim of the Trade Unions to participate on an equal footing in laying down the working conditions, under which their members are prepared to exercise skill and strength to their full capacity.

An industrial nation will probably have to come to terms with this shop floor scale of values, just as it has had to come to terms with the insurgent 'teen-age' style of life. There are also, I may add, indications that we shall soon have to deal with a pensioners' scheme of rights and values, now that so many well-preserved men are being retired about their mid-sixties. We are correct in referring to this shop floor style as essentially a middle age preserve, because in fact it had hitherto been mainly the men in their forties and over who set the stamp of approval or disapproval on what took place. Many of them recall the pre-war depression. Some of them are more or less contemporaries of the shop foremen, who tend to esteem highly what they regard as the older school of conscientious workers.

But there are no grounds for thinking that this state of affairs will continue. The weight of maximum influence could easily stretch back to the men in their thirties or twenties. Indeed, the accelerated technological changes favour such a shift. The teenager of today does not always shed his self-assurance when he enters the factory gates. For instance, the degree of uncertified absenteeism in some industries is probably less evident among middle-aged workers; and while I am not aware that unofficial strikes are commoner among the younger employees, the incidence of them suggests that there is an increasing break in *liaison* between the shop floor and the Unions. The middle-aged man is more prone by tradition to be a loyal and conventional Trade Unionist. Again, the established principle of 'seniority' in some industries seems to be falling into disuse; by seniority in this context is meant the safeguarding of a man's rights to promotion or of his right to be first in, last out, in cases of redundancy. The principle has less relevance where production methods are changing and labour is being deployed in new ways. Now that many executives in industry find themselves redundant or retired at a comparatively early age, the wage-worker in his fifties is looking more doubtfully at his prospects; and this makes him hesitate to compete with the younger voices he hears about him.

He may at this stage withdraw his mind more and more from any part he once took on the labour side in the affairs of the works. The chances are that he would always go along with his group. But if he ever had vague dreams of promotion he knows that he has now reached about as far up the ladder as he is likely to. He concentrates on getting through with the jobs of which, after all, he is a complete master; such boredom as they entailed in the past has probably become dulled with long experience. His changing family problems, his sporting and leisure interests etc. occupy more of his spare thoughts. If his work involves night shifts, the growing up and departure of children can often leave the wife in an uneasy or nervous state. The question arises of negotiating for transfer to a day job; and this itself might mean a smaller pay packet . . .

So run the courses of late middle age, with about as many variations as there are men. The solidarity of the 'club' still holds until a man retires; for the club or extended age group embodies all the accepted rights, proprieties, customs and mutual obligations of labour. It is far less arbitrary or spasmodic in its behaviour than is sometimes imagined by outsiders.

The growth of inner group cohesions among men or women on the job is simply due to the fact that, the more mechanized and potentially monotonous their work becomes, the more does satisfaction in working at all reside in the warm sense of being unified with one's mates, of forming part of a self-protecting fellowship with its own powers of decision. Relations with higher and lower management are, as I have said, a kind of 'game', the rules of which are tolerably well understood; there are or should be limits beyond which the legitimate demands of either side cannot be stretched.

If now for the sake of argument we define the middle-aged as those who fall somewhere between the ages of forty and sixty, we can get a fairly exact idea of the proportions they represent in the manual labour force. An examination of recent statistics published by the Ministry of Labour and by the Census Office suggests that in manufacture and mining they comprise today just about forty per cent of all male employees; that is to say, two in every five employed boys and men. In some industries, such as coal mining and iron and steel production, the proportion is nearer a half. Otherwise there is little to choose between one industry and another. The women workers are rather different. In several branches of manufacture the middle-aged do not account for much more than a third. But then, many women are disposed to withdraw from paid employment at a much earlier age than the men, especially where they are married women.

Figures of this kind show us momentarily the dimensions of the problem; but they need not be taken too seriously. For one thing, the age structure of a firm could change markedly with the passage of time. Industrial growth may mean a rapid recruitment of younger men; and alternatively a long-established firm may find itself burdened with an inconvenient proportion of middle-aged and still older men. In any case the mere *number* of the middle-aged in a working group does not tell us how much influence they exert in settling the pattern of duties and rights that the group as a whole is prepared to accept. That depends far more on the extent to which the younger men are willing to follow along the lines of conduct already laid down by their elders. These lines of conduct involve, it must be recalled, the attitudes towards management, the sense of tactics in a dispute, the element of group loyalty, the degree of respect or lack of respect for individual skill and efficiency, and many other factors. Collectively they bear some faint resemblance to what anthropologists often refer to as the 'culture' of a tribe or village. Though factory workers are far from being members of a primitive tribe, they have naturally inherited and developed their special *code of values*; and it is our business here to emphasize its importance in modern industry and to identify the variable part that the middle-aged play in it all.

The older executive

George Copeman

Dr George Copeman was born in 1922 and studied engineering. After the war he became interested in economics, and in 1953 he wrote a Ph.D. thesis on the careers of company directors. His main interest since then has been in management development. Two of his better known works are *The role of the Managing Director* and *Promotion and Pay for Executives.*

Dr Copeman is Managing Director of two companies in the Mercury House Group.

Anyone who advertises a professional or executive job without stating age limits is likely to find himself inundated with applications from men over 45. In the last few years technical change and company reorganizations have made thousands of them redundant. There were over 24,000 on the Executive and Professional Register of Unemployed at the end of 1966.

Some older executives never suffer from unemployment, in fact they go from strength to strength, while others become easy casualties. Why is this? Why should some be considered 'too old at forty' while others can say with satisfaction, 'Life begins at forty'?

The reasons are likely to be found in certain changes that occur during the Executive Life Cycle. The nature of an executive's work is such that, as he grows older, there are substantial changes in: (a) his Work Objectives; (b) his Earnings; (c) his Promotion Pattern; (d) his Required Skills.

Work objectives

A young man of potential managerial calibre usually begins his career with a professional or technical qualification or a degree, or some specialized skill such as salesmanship. He spends his early working years developing the one skill, which is likely to be concerned with a single aspect of business, such as production or marketing, personnel or finance. Only people who show that they have the ability to succeed in one specific skill-function are likely to be promoted to general management.

A young manager is, then, very much skill-oriented during his early career. He wants to become a better accountant, a better salesman, a better engineer, a better personnel man or whatever is appropriate.

Moreover, if he wants to make an original contribution to his profession by doing a piece of research, this is the most likely time he will do it and have it published against his own name. His professional pride, his desire for recognition by his 'peer group' of colleagues in the same profession, is at this time particularly high.

Proficiency at a skill does not, of course, bring full satisfaction unless it is applied usefully in the service of others. This becomes increasingly obvious to a young man as he rises to a responsible position in business. Whereas he may once have thought of professionalism for its own sake, now his satisfactions come from successfully meeting needs. In the business world, bent on serving customers, this means becoming customer-oriented. When he rises still higher in the organization he has to become more budget-conscious, more cost-conscious, more profit-conscious. He faces the stark fact that he can only go on giving satisfaction to customers if the revenue from customer purchases is at least as great as all the costs involved in providing them. So the more senior man looks at every existing product, every new product or project in terms of whether it is profitable now or is likely to be so in the future.

There is thus a natural progression for the successful manager from being almost entirely skill-oriented to being more and more customer-oriented, to becoming increasingly profit-oriented. This progression by itself explains why some older executives lose their jobs. They fall at either the first of these hurdles or the second. Usually their failure is not due to any decline in mental skill. Rather it is a matter of stagnation in personality development. They are unable to cope with the changes in attitude and behaviour necessary for higher business responsibility.

The single-minded devotion to a purpose, the self-discipline and ability to win the cooperation of others which are needed for any kind of success, even during the early stages of a career, are required much more intensely when a man rises above the level of laid-down policies, up into the rarefied atmosphere where he must both initiate plans and supervise their execution with nothing to guide him but his own built-in attitudes and behaviour patterns.

Earnings

A young man with professional or academic skills and with some ambition is, of course, deeply interested in salary progression. Though he knows that his usefulness to an employer at the start of his career is limited by lack of experience, as his experience increases he expects his salary to rise. It generally does, very substantially, and is likely to continue doing so for many years. By contrast a manual worker rises to his peak level of earnings by the time he is an adult.

The manner in which people with professional skills rise in salary with increasing age has been plotted on Earnings Progression Curves. The chart on the opposite page gives a typical picture of how some people rise faster than others, and those who rise very fast, the High Flyers, usually continue rising well into late middle age. By contrast those who rise slowly, the Steady Plodders, tend to stagnate in salary towards middle age.

Every professional worker has his own particular salary curve, which can be plotted. It has been found from the analysis of a large number of salary curves that those whose advancement is blocked and whose salary lags substantially behind the level appropriate for their age, are likely to become so frustrated that they seek and obtain another position.

Equally, those who are mistakenly promoted above their appropriate salary level are likely to be dismissed, or at least to have their salary frozen until they return to their proper progression curve.

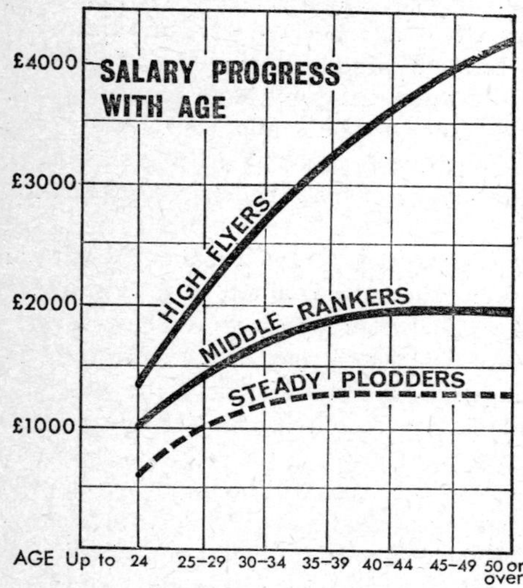

Thus it is broadly true to say that every manager has a natural rate of growth in usable abilities which determines the speed with which he becomes eligible for higher responsibilities and higher salary. It follows that too rapid promotion can be an executive's undoing, particularly in the later years when the curves for different types of people diverge so much. If for example, a man is really the type whose curve flattens out, and if he is mistakenly promoted as if his skills were still developing, he will almost certainly crash.

Promotion pattern

The maturing process in the executive life cycle is so significant that it also affects opportunities for re-engagement after a crash. In the hierarchy of a business organization there is an 'ideal' age-gap of about ten years between levels of authority. The relationship between two levels is facilitated if the junior man can respect the policy-making experience of his superior, and if the latter can respect the up-to-dateness and executing vigour of his subordinate. If the age-gap is about ten years, the superior is sufficiently older to have greater experience but not so old as to be fuddy-duddy in the eyes of his subordinate. Equally the younger man will have been educated and trained sufficiently later to be equipped with a more up-to-date set of principles and practices, yet be close enough to the background knowledge of his superior so that there is mutual understanding.

In practice age-gaps vary widely, but when they are neither too large nor too small they do facilitate the exercise of authority through the mutual respect they create. If, however, an executive loses his job – which may happen through no fault of his own, such as the failure of his firm – the generally accepted notion of age-gap makes it harder for him to find another post.

Most of the vacancies at his level will be filled by the promotion of younger men, thus giving opportunity and incentive to existing staff. Even if a post is filled from outside the firm, it may go to a younger man who is just coming up to the right level of experience and has some scope for salary growth before becoming expensive in the job.

If, to compete with these younger men, the redundant older man should decide to step down a grade or two, he will not necessarily find it easier. Employers will expect the more junior grade to be filled by people who are younger, more up-to-date professionally, easier to train, less fixed in personality and so more adaptable, easier to fit into the organization. So the difficulties of placing the older executive in a new job arise directly from the nature of the promotion pattern.

Required skills

We have seen how a manager who rises up the promotion

ladder is required to change his interests from their original concentration on professionalism towards interest in satisfying customer needs, and ultimately to profit-earning. In fact he has to change his skills as well as his interests. These changes can be greatly aided by good management training. But most managers do not receive any. They must adapt as they go along.

Some of them never fully adapt. The organization carries them and effectively shelters them from the need to adapt, so long as some of their colleagues are sufficiently attuned to the needs of the business. But when a crisis comes, such as a sudden drop in the company's market, those who have not adapted become more obvious passengers, unwanted people who are quickly thrown overboard.

There is nothing intrinsically difficult about the new skills which an executive must acquire as he rises in responsibility. Some of them are numerical skills, but for the vast majority of business problems they involve only simple arithmetic. In the few cases where advanced mathematics is required, the necessary expertise can be hired by the day from a consultant or an academic.

In addition to, even more important than numerical skills, of course, a senior manager requires a range of sophisticated communication skills plus certain self-disciplined attitudes and behaviour patterns. The traditional name for the full range of planning, controlling and communicating skills is 'leadership'. Though this is not generally a subject of study in the education system, it has not been entirely neglected outside the classroom.

The Duke of Wellington said that 'the Battle of Waterloo was won on the playing fields of Eton'. His simple message that leadership skills are developed by team games, is lost on many people because Eton happens to be symbolic of the education of one particular social class. Lord Baden-Powell also contributed to an understanding of the nature of leadership. His Scout movement imposes on the boys a continuing series of incentive tests and disciplines, plus a system of organization into small units of about six.

Modern research into leadership skills gives us some idea of just how much Wellington and Baden-Powell knew about their subject. Now, nearly every system of management training incorporates teamwork in its curriculum, whether by case preparation at Harvard, by syndicate work at Henley, business games or project exercises. But the vast majority of executives never have an opportunity to participate in such training. Hence they are vulnerable whenever the turn of economic events throws a spotlight on their deficiencies.

Few of the older executives who become redundant do so because of any decline in abilities. There is adequate medical evidence that people engaged in mental work do not usually decline in abilities until well past the normal retiring age.

What does happen quite frequently, however, is that they fail to continue the process of maturation, or personality development, required of a senior executive. It is for this reason that they become 'too old' at forty.

Marriage and the family in middle age

Dr Doris M. Odlum, M.A., M.R.C.S, L.R.C.P., D.P.M.

Dr Doris Odlum graduated from Oxford in Medicine and qualified at the Royal Free Hospital and St Mary's Hospital, London. She has been Consultant Psychiatrist and Consultant Physician for psychological medicine for several hospitals and is currently Vice President of the National Assoc. for Mental Health. She is the author of *Journey through Adolescence*, *Mind of Your Child*, besides numerous articles in the Medical Journals. Dr Odlum is 77.

For my purposes it is assumed that middle-age extends over the two decades from forty to sixty.

1. The early forties

In every country in the world the large majority of marriages take place before either party has reached the age of thirty, and the majority of children are born to parents in their third decade, that is to say, between the ages of twenty and thirty. This means that by the forties the family circle is usually complete including grandparents and other relations, and brothers and sisters and their children.

The close family ties that existed in former times have in many cases been loosened or even broken down by the migration of the younger people to big towns or new housing estates. This change has been accelerating during the last thirty years. It often gives rise to problems of loneliness and lack of parental and family support which add greatly to the stresses of young parents and especially the mother in the second and third decade.

By the time they have reached the forties however, they have mostly established themselves in their new setting and built up a circle of friends, mostly young married couples like themselves, with children of their own, so that they have a community of people on whom they can draw for companionship and mutual help. This may well provide a satisfactory compensation and has the advantage of enabling the young family to escape from the authoritarian control of the older generation and work out its own destiny on contemporary lines. The ideal is, of course, the preservation of family relationships and loyalties combined with independence and freedom for the young, and this situation is fortunately much more common today than it has ever been in the past.

THE MARRIAGE PATTERN

By the forties the majority of marriages have either stabilized or broken up, though there are a considerable number of separations and divorces between the years forty and fifty but they diminish markedly with increasing age. The pattern of the marriage is fixed for better or for worse. The storms and tempests of the earlier years have, for the most part, settled down into a relative calm which may be superficial but which suits both parties as providing a method of existence which is relatively satisfying and at any rate the best obtainable. They have learnt to know each other realistically and have lost the glamour and fantasy which, though delightful while it lasted, does not provide a satisfactory basis for day to day living. The differences in personality have been either accepted or at least are tolerated. The couple have achieved a circle of mutual friends and a community of interests or decided each to go their own way and seek what gratification they can apart from each other. Their sex life has developed into a routine which may or may not be mutually fulfilling. It is astonishing how often a woman accepts the fact that she does not get complete satisfaction or really enjoy her sex relationships without trying to improve this state of affairs. In most cases, however, she does not actually dislike sex and puts up with it or is even glad to feel that she is giving her husband pleasure. In a surprising number of cases husbands and wives never discuss their sex lives with each other and only too often the husband fails to realize that in fact his wife does not experience the full joy and satisfaction in their relationship which could be achieved if they had more mutual understanding.

At this stage the man may feel that intercourse with his wife has lost much of its emotional appeal. This is especially true if he has not learned how to arouse her desire and so does not obtain her full participation. It is one of the greatest hazards of marriage in middle age if one or both parties have become blasé or even bored with their sex-life.

Another problem is the fear of further pregnancies. This has undoubtedly been a nightmare to many women and has often made them refuse intercourse when otherwise they would have been quite willing or even happy to have it. Fortunately we are now at the dawn of a new era when this fear can be dispelled by the use of modern contraceptive methods and there is little doubt that in the long run it will lead to much happier and more stable marriages from many points of view.

One of the most important aspects of a marriage is the relationship with the in-laws and this also has usually settled down by the time the young couple have reached middle age and a more or less satisfactory compromise has been achieved. Only too often the early stages of marriage are complicated by the difficulty that the in-laws have in surrendering a beloved son or daughter. Jealousy on their part may go far to injure or even break up a marriage. On the other hand an immature boy or girl may well remain too dependent emotionally on one or other of their parents, most commonly the mother. By the time that the in-laws have become grandparents they can be a great help to the young couple and are usually much loved and valued by the children.

PARENTS AND CHILDREN

As has already been said the majority of children are born to parents of between twenty and thirty and therefore most families will be completed by the time that the parents are thirty-five or younger. On the whole they tend to have their children in fairly quick succession so that when the parents are in the early forties the children will include an age range of approximately eighteen to ten years.

The relationships between the parents and children and between the husband and wife as parents will have been firmly established for a good many years. The situation will therefore largely depend on what kind of family pattern has been built up. In the early forties the family group is still largely interdependent. Most of the children will still be at home and the close family group that exists before the children become adolescent will only now begin to show signs of breaking up.

Even in the most satisfactory families there is usually a phase of strained relationships between the children who are becoming adolescents and their parents. This stress begins to show itself by the time the children enter the pre-pubertal stage. In the British Isles this is approximately twelve or thirteen for girls and a little later for boys. The most difficult period usually seems to occur in girls between fourteen and seventeen and in boys between fifteen and eighteen with a peak for both between fifteen and sixteen. If the parents have developed a satisfactory relationship with each other the problems of adolescence may serve to bring them even more closely together. Indeed many adolescents appear to feel that the parents form a coalition against them. On the other hand if the marriage relationship has not been satisfactory it not infrequently happens that the woman has compensated for her frustrated marital situation by monopolizing the children and excluding the father, so that he has never played an active role in their lives. There are also a certain number of men who although they marry and have a family are not really suited to married life and feel no interest in their homes or their children. From an early age the children themselves are of course well aware of the relationship and emotional tensions between their parents and also between each parent and themselves. Children are extremely sensitive to the emotional atmosphere in the home and especially to any tension between their parents. In adolescence when they particularly need parental support because of their personal insecurity it is extremely important that the home should provide a calm and stable environment. This is essentially a time when in the course of their normal development children become more critical and begin to look at their family and the world around them objectively. This means that they will be comparing and contrasting their own home and family pattern with those of their friends. Children do in fact idealize their parents to a remarkable degree when they are younger and the inevitable re-appraisal on a more realistic basis, even under the best conditions, usually presents them with a distressing conflict. It is vitally important for their satisfactory psychological development that they should be able to feel respect for their parents and to retain their confidence in them.

When the situation in the home is satisfactory even the storms and tensions of adolescence do no more than shake the family temporarily and in the later stages of the parents' middle age, when the children are themselves marrying and settling down and establishing families of their own, they are only too glad to return, as it were, to the family and appreciate and value the love and help that their parents can give them.

2. *The great divide*

By the age of forty-five we reach what might be termed 'the great divide', that is to say, the stage when we have arrived at the end of our youth and developmental phase and are entering into the involutional phase.

Most people find about this time of life that they have to do some stocktaking. The realization comes that they are no longer young and that the doors of opportunity are closing. No longer are they able to feel that anything is possible. Their lives are established in more or less of a rut and in reviewing their situation and achievement they are fortunate if they do not feel some sense of failure and frustration. Both parties may well ask themselves, 'Has my marriage turned out to be all that I hoped and wished?' The man will think. 'Am I in the job that I wanted to do? Is my status relative to my colleagues satisfactory? Can I improve my position or at least maintain my present one? What have I got to look forward to in the years ahead?'

THE CHANGING PATTERN

In many jobs, especially those involving severe physical effort or speed, both men and women are less efficient when they reach the middle forties than they were previously and this decline will inevitably be progressive. In occupations which require skill and mental alertness however, experience and increased stability may more than compensate for a number of years for any deterioration due to ageing. Indeed, people in the higher categories usually obtain their most responsible jobs in the late forties and carry on into the middle sixties. It is vitally important for anyone in a professional or executive job to achieve promotion before fifty, otherwise there is little chance that he or she will get further and this may induce a sense of frustration and failure. In the case of a woman whose life in the large majority of cases centres round her family the stocktaking may be somewhat depressing. She realizes that she is losing the physical attraction of her youth. She has to face the fact that her partly unconscious fantasies of being attractive to men and her ideal of her own beauty is fading and she may well fear that this may make her husband cease to be interested in her and seek the company of other women. From forty-five onwards the children will no longer be so dependent on her and the older ones will probably have married or at any rate want to live their own lives. Even those who are still at home do not really need her as a person, only as a background. One of the commonest complaints of the women in the late forties is that they are taken for granted, that no-one is interested in them as individuals. They feel that they are the family drudge and not expected to have any personal interests or desires. Nobody listens to their opinions and nobody does anything to give them pleasure or make life easier for them. The children expect to bring their friends in at all hours and to find adequate food and drink available. Their husbands spend the evening reading the paper and watching television and seldom want to talk to their wives. It is rare for a husband to suggest taking his wife out for an evening's pleasure. If she suggests that he should do so he may grudgingly agree but, as so many women say, it would make all the difference if only the husband were the initiator. On the other hand husbands and wives do go out together more than they used to. He is usually quite pleased if she is prepared to accompany him, for a drink in the pub in the evening or when he is gratifying his own interests by attending a football match, but this is rather a different matter.

It is usually in the middle forties that women begin to wish to take up some new interest or activity. Today, as we know, the expectation of life for women and men is much increased and not only life but health and energy, both mental and physical. A woman of between forty-five and sixty is well able in most cases to take an active part in the life of the community. Even if she has not had any previous training there are many jobs both paid and unpaid in which she can be extremely valuable.

It is now fairly generally accepted that it is a good thing for the older woman to do this. The Victorian idea that the woman should devote her entire life to her husband's needs and comforts or that it was a humiliation for him to let it be known that he could not entirely support his wife are completely out of date and even where there is no economical necessity for the middle-aged woman to work it is regarded as desirable that she should have some occupation and interest both from the point of view of the community and of her own well being.

3. *The involutional phase*

Not only women, but also many men undergo a period of physical and psychological instability between forty-five and fifty-five. The disturbances associated with the menopause in women are today mitigated by the use of hormones and in any case appear to be much less severe than they were fifty years ago in the large majority of cases. Few women however, entirely escape some physical discomfort and some psychological disturbance during this phase. The commonest psychological disturbances take the form of increased tension and irritability, a mild degree of depression, a tendency to tire easily, and not infrequently a decrease in sexual desire and interest. These are more marked in what corresponds to the pre-menstrual phase. In the old days the whole subject was extremely hush-hush and its causation little understood. The woman was often blamed for her apparent ill humour or inadequacy and the husband thought that she was being unreasonable or had even ceased to love him. In the male, menopausal symptoms also tend to take the form of depression associated with irritability and tension, but they are more diffuse and less cyclical in character and he does not have to endure the physical discomforts that women go through. It has only relatively recently been appreciated that these symptoms in a man do in fact correspond with the change of life in women.

A not uncommon phenomenon in men at this stage is what might be regarded as almost a second adolescence. This takes the form of heightened sexual interest in much younger women coupled with the desire to prove themselves as still potent and attractive. The type of emotion they experience is as glamorous and unrealistic as that of the adolescent boy of sixteen or seventeen, and their behaviour is often completely irrational. It is interesting that those women who pass through a somewhat similar phase tend to prefer a man of their own age or slightly older and relatively rarely become involved with a much younger one; possibly in some cases this is due to lack of opportunity. This phase occurs however, much more rarely in women than in men. If it does occur to either spouse the future of the marriage depends to a great extent on the attitude adopted by the other partner. If he or she can accept it the situation in the majority of cases readjusts itself in two or three years. The emotional maturity of the aggrieved partner is, therefore, often the deciding factor. If he or she regards the spouse's behaviour as an unforgivable personal affront, adopts a childish self-pitying attitude or tries to punish the erring spouse by constant nagging and quarrelling or publicizes their problems among their friends the marriage either breaks up or degenerates into a cohabitation of people who are resentful or hostile to each other. Unfortunately since this occurs at the menopausal stage both parties may be in a state of instability which makes them less able to face the situation in a calm or rational manner. If a marriage does survive an episode of this kind, however, it not infrequently leads to a greater depth of affection and understanding between the partners.

When a marriage breaks up for this reason the aggrieved man is far more likely to enter into relations with another woman than the aggrieved wife with another man; partly because she does not desire it and partly, no doubt, because there have been in the past fewer men available than there are women to fill the rôle of comforter. As there are now more men in the twenties than women and therefore very few women will be likely to remain unmarried this source of gratification for men looks like drying up in the future.

4. The later years

By the middle fifties the family situation has usually settled down satisfactorily.

In a number of cases however, the couple may be faced with the problem of their own ageing parents, who may well be infirm or one of whom may have died. Most older people want to continue to live independently and very much dislike having to share a home with their children. The children themselves may find it extremely difficult to share with elderly parents, especially if there are still young people living at home, since the older generation are often out of sympathy with the young and the young are impatient of the old. Many modern houses, also, are very small and there is not adequate room for the old parents or parent to have any separate accommodation. It is sometimes said that the middle-aged are less willing today to have the care of their elderly parents than they used to be but recent investigations show that a very high proportion of the elderly and infirm are living with their children, often under conditions which produce considerable stress in the family and press particularly heavily on the mother.

After the menopause, which in practically all women in the western world is completed by fifty-five, women are often healthier than they have been for a number of years previously and their expectation of life now extends to the middle seventies. On the other hand the vulnerability of men increases from fifty onwards and a man's expectation of life is nearly five years less, that is to say, approximately sixty-nine years. The graph of morbidity of men and women crosses in favour of the woman, in the fifties. The majority of women give up their paid jobs by sixty, which is the official retiring age, but are still alert and active and many of them carry on with voluntary work.

Most men in the late fifties are beginning to look forward to their retirement. The high morbidity and mortality rate of men between fifty and sixty is certainly a matter for serious concern and many women who are widowed at this time have to face the problem of making a new life for themselves. Deprived of a beloved partner and the security of their home, often in straightened circumstances and with declining powers, they have little hope of obtaining paid work and dread being dependent. But the love and support of their children in the majority of cases enables them to make a fairly satisfactory adjustment.

The role of the grandmother today

Ruth Adam

Ruth Adam, herself a grandmother, is a professional writer who has contributed to a large number of periodicals and newspapers. She has written a good deal of fiction as well as some school text books and a biography.

In the second half of the twentieth century there are more grandparents about than ever before and they have a longer run in the role than any of their predecessors. This – the most married generation in history – tends to have its children earlier, which provides more grandparent parts, and more people survive to fill them. In 1900 a woman of 20 could expect to live for another forty-six years; now she can expect another fifty-five.

Increased expectation of life which, so far as the individual is concerned 'can't be bad' is liable to be received by the community, as such, with gloom and foreboding. Governments point out the mounting burden on the exchequer of the increase in the number of old-age pensions which will have to be paid out. The Beveridge Report, which laid down so much of the pattern of our life today was less than generous to the old, because he anticipated that the pensionable age-group would grow, during the next thirty years, from twelve per cent of the population to twenty-one per cent. The post-Beveridge community is agreed on the 'dependency' of the child up to the age of eighteen and of the old person after sixty. If the old are going to stay around so much longer than they used to, it means an increasing financial drain on all those in the middle of their life-span who are supporting those at the two ends of it. They are most conscious of the individual burden within the family. People on a pension of any kind are, by definition, poorer than they were before and need varying degrees of help, ranging from board and lodging and nursing down to an occasional car-ride. When they become physically dependent there are not enough beds and attendants to go round either privately or in public care. All this makes old age rather like the point in a party at which you notice your hosts beginning to glance surreptitiously at the clock.

The only role in which an old person has an intrinsic value is as a grandparent. You can acquire a new husband or wife, but your grandfather or grandmother cannot be replaced. The grandparent has a unique emotional relationship with the youngest generation. In a culture which thinks and talks more about 'love' and 'youth' than any other aspects of human existence, this puts grandparents in a very strong position indeed. They do the baby a favour merely by existing. If they can make a success of the relationship during the coming years they can rely on being genuinely mourned when it is over.

Realizing that one has a new value in late middle age accounts for the current social status of becoming a grandparent. In the twenties, Sinclair Lewis's globe-trotting heroine, in *Dodsworth* begged her husband to keep the birth of their first grandchild a secret. 'Don't you realize that all our friends in Europe think of me as young? And if they know I'm a grandmother – God – a grandmother! It's horrible. It's the end for me! A grandmother! Lace caps and knitting and rheumatism.'

The reluctant grandmother would be incomprehensible today, since the popular concept of one is not necessarily that of an old woman. The span between grandparent and grandchild is shorter than it was even so recently as the twenties, because the average age for marriage has gone down sharply, and in any case since the grandmother has used up not much more than two-thirds of her own span yet, she registers as younger than she did when the average woman could look forward to a bare twelve years in the chimney-corner after her youngest child was off her hands. Apart from this, the birth of a grandchild moves her up into a new social rank, reserved for those who have this visible proof of a successful love-life of their own, and of raising children who also have one. In fact there comes a point in one's fifties and early sixties when the non-grandparent is pitiable in exactly the way an 'old maid' used to be in the days when there were superfluous women in the marrying age-group. 'Never mind, I daresay *you'll* have one soon,' say her friends consolingly, when she gets left out of the grandchild-comparing conversation.

But since even the role of parents is now sufficiently in doubt to be continually discussed in family journals and television programmes, it would be surprising if the grandmother of today was absolutely clear about hers. Should she aim at being the authoritative, disciplinary one of Victorian tradition? When Lady Stanley of Alderley had her grandchildren to stay, she wrote to their mother:

> 'Children very well, but they are not half as agreeable company as they were a year ago, so very silly and giggling over things they *know* they ought not to say – and Rosalind is not at all *truthful* – I am sure you ought to attend to this point – she is so very cunning and artful – and Algernon is very *dirty* in his ideas – bad company for a sister and should be looked after very closely.'

In 1851, her daughter-in-law, though she grumbled privately to her husband about it, never questioned the old lady's right to lay down the law. But in the nineteen-twenties a social revolution which was more violent and effective than any before it – or since – disposed of the disciplinary grandmother and she has never reappeared. After the 1914–18 war, adolescents and young adults rebelled against the now discredited traditions of their elders and escaped from home into the outside world. They took to eating in restaurants and consorting only with their contemporaries and treating marriage lightly. The ideal family size was 'one child and a car.' At the same time there was a revolution in baby-care which we have been extending, though not fundamentally changing, ever since. My own grandmother used to sniff over the modern ideas of my mother – for instance in not allowing 'dummies' and conceding that bed-wetting was not intentional – but they talked the same language about child upbringing. But my mother's first grandchild was a 'Truby King' baby, with a fixed formula of sleep and measured vitamins and pasteurized milk which was so much Greek to its grandparents. The laughable ignorance of grandmothers about the way to raise a baby was one of the standing jokes of the twenties. It knocked the grandmother off her pedestal as the embodiment of maternal wisdom and her stock remained low right up to the fifties.

She has had a second role, however, since the beginning of time, as a reserve line of defence for the third generation. You find her in fairy-tales, such as Hans Andersen's *The Little Match-Girl*. In it, the grandmother who has cared for the orphan is dead and she herself is dying of cold and starvation. She strikes away her stock to warm herself, and in the light of the burning matches sees a vision of the grandmother coming to fetch her. This protective grandmother was hard hit by the foundation of the Welfare State, with its safety-net of community care for deprived children, which took away much of the grandmother's function. It also took over her dramatic duty as the rescuer of the household hit by a domestic emergency – a birth or the illness of the mother. Now there were (or at least there were planned to be) Local Authority Home Helps to be summoned, and 'short-stay Homes' for the older children if the mother went to hospital.

But the first years of the scheme which was to provide cradle-to-grave security were marked by a peak number of insecure children. By 1954 there were over sixty-five thousand of them deprived of family background and in public care and the divorce rate was four times greater than it had been before the war. At this point, the social workers who had been taking the centre of the stage and pushing the grandmother into the wings had to turn to her for help. Since parents persisted in putting their own love-life before their parental duties and going off with other partners, the only hope of a stable relationship for their children lay in the 'extended' family in which relatives would feel an obligation to take over, as they always have done in Jewish families. Grandmothers – particularly of illegitimate grandchildren – became much in demand.

What really put the grandmother on the map was the study of *Family and Kinship in East London* by Michael Young and Peter Wilmott. It not only became a classic, but started a school of similar studies. It revealed a warm, dynamic family life in which the three generations were closely knit. Married daughters lived on their mother's doorstep and looked after her, while she, in return, looked after the grandchildren. This book made a tremendous impression. The Bethnal Green grandmother became the ideal prototype for middle-aged and elderly women among the intelligentsia in Hampstead, commuters' wives in Gerrards Cross and in the stockbroker belt of Surrey. When the East End communities were broken up under slum-clearance schemes and their inhabitants moved to new towns, with a two-generation population, they found family life arid, and the Sunday expedition to visit grandparents no substitute for everyday proximity. Recently, there has been a move to build housing units in new developments specifically for old people.

The cult of the Bethnal Green grandmother suffered a setback as the number of married women going out to work rose steadily and available domestic help shrank. 'The young expect their parents to take their place with the children as a matter of course,' grumbled one grandmother, whose own stretch as full-time housewife had begun in the days of ration-books and evacuees and who had only recently begun to taste the sweets of liberty from it. Now she found herself back in the old rut, with diaper-pails in the bathroom again, having to change her library-book by proxy and the old five-o'clock exhaustion. When you have welcomed your promotion to grandmotherhood with awe and satisfaction, it is disillusioning to be regarded simply as unpaid baby-minder. In any case, the grandmother may have ideas about returning to the labour-market herself.

According to the East London tradition, baby-minding and getting tea for the school-age child is a return for help given by the second generation to the old. But the middle-class and still middle-aged grandparents have not, so far, needed any help. At this stage of their life, with children off their hands but their income not yet shrunk to pension-size, they are probably in easier circumstances than ever before. They receive demands but make none. All the same, it is during these first years of the grandparent situation, when love is expressed by actual service to the grandchild, in which the foundation of the future relationship is laid. Nothing that comes later can establish it in the same way. And there are two periods of being a grandparent. Now, the grandparent is independent and the grandchild totally dependent, but later on the position will be reversed. The relationship to teenager and young adult can be the most rewarding of all.

It includes what the anthropologist calls 'privileged disrespect between alternate generations.' Grandparents, by tradition indulge their grandchildren more than they did their own children, since they no longer have the same vested interest in day-to-day discipline and since there is no competition between alternate generations, as there is between adjacent ones. 'Good old Nan, she's my pal. She's a good old girl,' said one of the Bethnal Green grandchildren. This social equality is perhaps part of the special affinity between today's teenager and old-age-pensioner. The headmistress of a large south-London secondary modern school says that her senior girls will give up time, effort and money to voluntary work – provided that it is something to do with 'old folks', but on no other condition. They like to make personal friends among lonely ones. At a youth club in an inner-London district, where plans for any wedding-party are discussed in detail, for months beforehand, the presence and function of the grandmother at the wedding is accepted as important. At this moment of embarking on a new family unit, your roots matter. The grandmother as a source of tiny gifts and 'treats' is so deeply embedded in tradition that part of the uneasiness of the woman who finds herself cast as permanent baby-minder is because this cancels out the role of the indulgent one. If you have to look after children regularly you are bound to become the upholder of discipline instead of the person who delightfully flaunts it.

The present grandparent generation is well equipped for another traditional role – that of being a personal link with history – because no group of human beings has ever before seen so many changes in the course of a single lifetime. They could leave Robert Southey's famous 'Old Caspar' standing at the starting-post. When his 'little grandchild Wilhelmine' found a skull he was able to supply her with an eye-witness account of the Battle of Blenheim, though he fell down when asked to diagnose the causes of war. ('Why that I cannot tell,' said he; But 'twas a famous victory.') Old Caspar grandfather-figures have had an unprecedented run on television lately, describing what it felt like to be in the trenches in 1916. (They have slightly spoiled the market for the amateur in the home circle.) Grandmothers do better as a link-with-history in novels and have inspired a whole school of fiction. The best-known example is that of 'old Adeline' in the Whiteoaks saga. The respect she gets from all her descendants is based on the fact that she was the original pioneer of the family, who emigrated to Canada and founded the Jalna estate on which they all live. The standard pattern of this school of fiction makes the climax of the story the grandmother's hundredth birthday. Before she dies – on it – she has supplied her favourite great-grandchild with some piece of philosophy, from her own long experience, which enables him to sort out his own problems.

The popular image of the late-twentieth-century grandmother can best be seen in radio and television soap-operas about family life. 'Doris Archer' of the long-running radio serial about farming people, for instance, draws on most of the traditional roles at one time or another. She is by turns the disciplinary grandmother – lecturing her illicitly-pregnant granddaughter severely; the indulgent one – who was appealed to by the granddaughter for sympathy; and the protective one – who finally offered to take over the confinement because the parents were occupied with their own business. But neither she nor any other grandmother of current folk-lore is ever represented as a senior-citizen, altruistic grandmother, whose broadened sympathies have made her more detached from personal interests, 'in calm of mind, all passion spent.'

Juvenile court magistrates have to be parent-age, not grandparent-age, and although a grandfather may find his position an asset on a Youth Service committee, the same thing does not apply to the grandmother (possibly because there have always been Elder Statesmen but no Elder Stateswomen). Earlier in life, the experience of motherhood was accepted as producing an immediate width of feeling and outlook, presuming that the mother thinks, 'How would I feel if this child was one of my own?' Grandmotherhood is not expected to extend the heart's understanding any further. On the contrary 'grandmotherly' is a term for particular narrowness and lack of enlightenment, as in 'grandmotherly legislation'. And yet if having grandchildren is an emotional experience, and a less possessive one than any other at that, the altruistic grandmother is exactly what it might be expected to produce; a woman who can look, without fear, towards the time when she will be dead, to whom every schoolchild without a fair chance, every neglected baby and every war orphan matters, because they are all, by proxy, her own grandchildren.

Index